"The business book for the 21st century! My head bobbed up and down in agreement as I read through this page turner. Few business books have provided me with the insights and practical knowledge as I found here."

HANK STROLL, PUBLISHER, *PROFESSIONAL SERVICES JOURNAL*
WWW.INTERNETVIZ.COM

"A timely topic for both product and services companies of all sizes. Backed by current global research and real-life experience of the authors, the book is a valuable guide for all executives and managers trying to improve margins and compete with total solutions competitors."

JIM PRITCHETT, CEO, PETRIS TECHNOLOGY

"Outstanding! *S-Business* is must reading for anyone serious about building a high-performance services organization."

LIZ MURPHY, VICE PRESIDENT, PROFESSIONAL SERVICES, DATATEL

"Alexander and Hordes have written the book on S-Business! This book is a must read for anyone in the services business. I highly recommend it to all industry leaders."

JOHN SCHOENEWALD, CEO AFSM INTERNATIONAL
(THE GLOBAL ASSOCIATION FOR THE SERVICES INDUSTRY)

"Mark Hordes and Jim Alexander have done a terrific job at both capturing the distinctive characteristics of S-Businesses and providing very useful insights on how to 'make the leap'. Their insights are applicable to a broad range of businesses, whether they be biased toward the 'pure service' end of the spectrum or not."

DAVID DOVE, PRESIDENT, DOVE CONSULTING

"The authors have captured the dramatic shift increasingly required for successful businesses—that being they must become services enterprises. More importantly, the book offers a practical and powerful framework for achieving exceptional performance following a step-by-step, hands on process."

STEPHEN W BROWN, PHD, PROFESSOR AND DIRECTOR
CENTER FOR SERVICES LEADERSHIP, W A CAREY SCHOOL OF BUSINESS
ARIZONA STATE UNIVERSITY, TEMPE, ARIZONA

"*Reinventing the Services Organization* is must reading for any executive in the services industry. This is especially true for executives and managers at product-centric companies trying to make the challenging transition to a services focused business. Jim and Mark provide invaluable insights consisting of both knowledge and real world experience that will be extremely helpful regardless of your specific industry segment."

DONALD L. PETERS, VICE PRESIDENT OF MANAGED SERVICES
FUJITSU TECHNOLOGY SOLUTIONS, INC.

"Alexander and Hordes have provided a genuine and timely must read book for all S-Business advocates and for those who have not yet seen the way. As service continues to become the focus point of today's successful businesses, *S-Business:Reinventing the Services Organization*, is what each manager needs to approach the question of where are we and how do we successfully transform our approach. These gentlemen have given us a real road map, which allows us to understand our current position, what we must do to move to the next level and what tools we can use. This is an outstanding business book and should be on each manager's must read list. I highly recommend their book as a powerful tool in helping you formulate your transition to a services led company."

DENNIS GERSHOWITZ, VICE PRESIDENT SERVICE OPERATIONS
ALFA WASSERMANN, INC.

"This is a must read for anyone involved in business today. The authors force us to challenge our old models and success formulas for how service organizations work and operate. This is an instructive and thought provoking road map to transforming an organization to a services led s-business."

ROBERT MORGAN, PRESIDENT
HUMAN CAPITAL CONSULTING GROUP, SPHERION CORPORATION

"Terrific read, loaded with great ideas. Buy a copy for everyone in your organization—they'll all profit from it."

STEVE M. WINTER, PRINCIPAL/CEO, ERGOS TECHNOLOGY PARTNERS, INC.

"The Chapter on Talent alone is worth its weight in gold! As a firm that focuses on the Human Capital market place this is a terrific read for anyone who is interested in developing their professional services business and people."

"This book is the most useful and thorough book I have ever come across. Forget your MBA, this book will provide you with a complete road map for successfully changing, creating and operating any company that aspires to the high margin and highly valued services business. In particular, *S-Business:Reinventing the Services Organization* is an excellent portrayal of the critical business challenges companies in the computer industry face in moving to a highly valued services model. It is packed with insightful information and instruction on all aspects of the organizational change necessary to get there. This book has provided us with more clarity and refinement to effectively create this change than our organization has formulated in the many years we have been struggling with to reach the level of success we aspire to. This book will be a business saver, it will not only show you how to become an s-business but also ensure you set your expectations correctly so you know what level and type of s-business business you should be."

"With hands on experience and a professional approach, the book provides usable information, models, and checklists based on real experience. I am impressed. There is no way this book cannot help every service company. Love the best practices checklist that separates the elite from everyone else. This can help put in place the framework to build a more profitable business and competitive advantage. The strategic analysis is very thorough and well thought out. Executives trying to align their management team on the future direction of s-business can utilize the framework for understanding the success levers. I have used it with some of key executives and it works! Profound and insightful layout of the 'service marketing principles', and the 'best practices with People'. I have already passed it on to our top leaders as a road map to get us there!"

S-BUSINESS

S-BUSINESS
Reinventing the
Services Organization

**James A. Alexander
and Mark W. Hordes**

SelectBooks, Inc.

S-Business: Reinventing the Services Organization
©2003 James A. Alexander and Mark W. Hordes

This edition published by SelectBooks, Inc.
For information address SelectBooks, Inc., New York, New York.

First Edition

ISBN 1-59079-054-5

Library of Congress Cataloging-in-Publication Data

Alexander, James A.
  S-business : reinventing the services organization / James A. Alexander,
Mark W. Hordes.—1st ed.
     p. cm.
  Includes bibliographical references and index.
  ISBN 1-59079-054-5
  1. Service industries—Management. I. Hordes, Mark W. II. Title.
HD9980.5.A43 2003
658.4'012—dc21

2003005078

Manufactured in the United States of America

10 9 8 7 6 5 4 3 2 1

To my best friend Janny

James A. Alexander

To Vivian, my ongoing source of inspiration

Mark W. Hordes

Contents

Introduction

Purpose of the Book

The purpose of this book is to provide the business leaders of traditional product-centered companies and existing services organizations with a succinct, yet comprehensive blueprint to rethink and reinvent their services businesses (s-businesses, for short). Readers of this book will:

- Understand s-business and it's huge potential
- Determine if s-business is the correct business approach for their organizations
- Compare global, research-based standards against their organizations' performance to target high-potential opportunities
- Harness the "core" and statistically proven "best practices" of star performing s-businesses to focus and guide performance improvement
- Learn the special challenges of services and the unique s-business strategies and approaches required to market, sell, and deliver services and solutions effectively

1

- Discover the process and key steps required to make the transition from a product-centered organization to a services-led s-business
- Institute appropriate organizational changes to optimize the s-business potential

Cannily done, the result is services reinvention and significant competitive advantage.

S-Business Definition

But what is s-business? Let's first determine what it is not. S-business is not consultant-speak for the important but well-worn philosophy of customer service. Enough has been said on this topic. Nor is s-business a substitute jargon referring to the professional services field.

The term *s-business* refers to the services-focused, services-measured, and, indeed, services-driven organization, regardless of whether it also builds and sells products

Who Will Benefit from Reading This Book?

There is a direct application of the contents of this book to anyone who has an interest in and the responsibility for using services to improve the performance, profitability, and market potential of his/her enterprise:

- Senior-level executives responsible for organization strategy and tasked with contributing significant gains in shareholder value
- Executives and managers responsible for implementing services, professional services, and total solution initiatives in their organizations and tasked with contributing new and profitable revenue
- Professionals in management consulting, technology consulting, and strategy firms
- Organizational change agents
- Services professionals from all industries

Our Approach

This book is built upon two equally important inputs: practical research coupled with first-hand experience.

A first of its kind, recently completed global research project (Alexander, 2002) laid the foundation for validating s-business—defining financial benchmarks, quantitatively comparing s-business with product-centered companies, defining the best practices of high-performing services-driven businesses, and uncovering the transition levers of top-performers. These findings frame our recommendations, and highlights of the research are integrated into the text throughout the book.

Yet the research is tempered by the practical. Both authors of this book have spent many years in the services industry learning (sometimes painfully) what works and what doesn't. Client engagements have provided many of the practical ideas reported in the following pages. This view "from the trenches" provides the reality check required when confronted with the latest seemingly elegant theory or a newly crafted four-box matrix.

Finally, we have tried desperately to make this book reader-friendly: easy to read, succinct, and immediately actionable. Because at the end of the day, it's all about improving performance.

A Global Trend

Over the last fifteen years a significant business trend has been occurring that still is under the radar screen of the business press. It's a shift that is not as flashy as disruptive Internet technologies and e-business, not as sexy as globalization or learning organizations, not as dramatic as corporate mergers or business process reengineering. Yet the steady, on-going movement in the importance of services to an organization's portfolio of offerings and its resulting impact on business performance may be more important strategically than any of the initiatives mentioned above. This is the new world of s-business.

Led (sometimes dragged) by customer demands and the realities of an increasingly competitive marketplace, select organizations in all categories are changing the emphasis of their businesses from products to services. IBM and GE are high-profile examples of organizations that have already accomplished this transition to s-business. Formerly product-centered organizations selling big boxes and providing product-support services on request, they are now services-driven businesses that *push* the value of their services offerings and *pull* along their tangible products. As a result, today IBM Global Services generates more than $33 billion in annual revenue and employs over half the corporation's workforce.

But it is not only the traditional product-centered companies that are interested in s-business. Professional services firms such as Accenture and McKinsey are increasing their marketing and delivery capabilities and creating new alliances to meet the ever-expanding, ever-demanding issues and needs of customers and clients. Furthermore, as the demand for more robust services increases, all segments of the economy will be touched by s-business. No organization of any size, in any market or geography, can afford not to implement an s-business strategy. The stakes are just too high. No matter what an organization's past portfolio of offerings, today's drivers of success depend upon knowing how to organize, lead, and manage a services-led enterprise.

What's the Value?

The services potential for most all product organizations is immense. Gary Bridge, former senior vice president and futurist at IBM, has stated that for every $1 of software sold, $162 is paid out in services—and IBM wants its (more than) fair share. Earlier consulting work by the authors of this book has demonstrated that on average a three- to seven-fold increase in revenues can be expected when services are systematically added to the offerings portfolio. In addition, recent groundbreaking research by one of the authors (Alexander, 2002) on 370 companies in twenty-nine countries showed that today services have average gross margins more than 50% higher than products and the current annual growth rate of services is more than double that of products, with a significant acceleration planned within two years. Finally, this same research study revealed that top performers are *averaging 61% gross margins and a 30% annual growth rate* for their services offerings. These elite "s-businesses" (organizations that push services to pull products) have broken the code when it comes to dramatically delivering new streams of revenue and increased profitability by creating and selling what customers are demanding—more and better services.

What's So Different About Services?

There is an extreme difference between products and services. First of all, in most cases, the products produced by traditional organizations can be easily seen, felt, and described. However, services are intangible. Evert Gummesson probably said it the most eloquently, stating that "services are something that can be bought and sold but can't be dropped on your foot" (Gummesson, 1999, p. 11). The challenge of dealing with the added complexity of intangibility alone raises the bar.

In addition, some other major differences between the two types of offerings, as shown in Figure 1, are worth noting.

Figure 1: What's so different about services?

Dimension	Products	Services
Production	Built	Performed
Production goal	Uniformity	Uniqueness
Involvement	Rarely	Usually
Quality control	Compare outputs to specs	Compare customer expectations to experience
Poor quality procedure	Recall	Apologize and atone
Morale and skill level	Important	Vital

These distinctions have a fundamental impact on how one produces, markets, sells, delivers, supports, and measures the performance of services and the success of the s-business itself. What may have worked extremely well in managing a traditional product-based organization will be ineffective in the world of services.

Several people have helped distinguish between "products" and "services" (Schwartz, 1992; Zemke, 1992). Through experience we have learned that trying to produce and manage services the same way that one produces and manages products doesn't work. There are some fundamental differences.

Production

Products are built. The computers and printers that the computer reseller offers are all manufactured and assembled on the production lines of hardware manufacturers in highly controlled environments. They are physically molded, soldered, inserted, welded, glued, assembled, and boxed. Products can be directly experienced and tested prior to usage. Features can be seen and functions can be observed. The customer owns an object.

Services are performed. Services are delivered live, in real time, usually at the customer's location. In many instances products are involved, but it is the service provider who is "on-stage." The customer's perceptions are based upon the actual actions of the service provider. When the computer reseller personnel go out to a customer location to install a computer network, what the customer sees is a performance. The customer owns an experience.

Goals

The production goal of products is uniformity. Variation must be controlled. The manufacturers of computer hardware strive to have all of their equipment perform in exactly the same way. The computer reseller depends/hopes that all models work the same way. The reseller assumes that parts from one model number work on another unit of the same model number. The product is generic.

The goal of performing services is more complicated. Although the process of delivering a service such as on-site equipment repair or systems integration may be the same, the successful services provider makes the experience unique to the specific customer. The actual *process* of performing a service may (and probably should) stay the same, but variation is required to meet the uniqueness of the customer and the situation. The services offering must be personalized.

Customer Involvement

With products, the customer is rarely involved in production. Production could occur in the next county or the next country. For the most part, the customer doesn't care. The purchasers of the products sold by the computer reseller don't know or care whether their computers were manufactured in Texas or Brazil. The closest the computer reseller may have been to being involved in production might have been a visit to the manufacturer, taking a tour of the production facility.

With services, the customer is often involved in the service performance. In many cases, the service is performed up close and personal. Because of this, the customer is often involved in the actual performance. Each customer interprets things differently. Since the services performers are right there, on-stage, they are often subject to special requests that may not be a part of the original agreements.

Quality Control

In the production of products, quality control is straightforward. The outputs of the production process are compared to standardized specifications. Smart manufacturers have built robust practices to build quality in, and to check quality at each point in the production process. The manufacturer defines quality. The computer reseller looks at the quality of the goods it buys and sells by performance versus manufacturer claims, reliability (such as MTBF, or *mean time between failures)*, and the number of DOAs *(dead on arrivals)*. When products are improperly produced, they can be identified through inspection or recalled from the field. The manufacturer of defective printers could substitute a printer with the same, similar, or greater capabilities.

In services, quality control is conducted by the customer. The customer keeps the specifications in his/her head. The customer compares the service experience to the expectations developed prior to the performance. Unlike products that rarely change specifications, services customer expectations are much more fluid. In fact, customer expectations often change during the performance of a service, adding to the complexity of the performance. Although the computer reseller may sell exactly the same service to two similar appearing businesses in the same field, each will define quality differently. When services are improperly performed, apologies and reparations are the only means of recourse. A poor performance is usually discovered immediately. The customer of the computer reseller knows immediately after the training session "whether the training was any good." Even if the reseller refunds the money or offers to provide the training again, the damage has been done.

Morale and Skills

The morale and skills of production workers are important. Qualified workers with good attitudes improve efficiency and increase the likelihood of producing high-quality products.

The morale and skill of service performers are critical. They perform during moments of truth in real time at the customer's location. They must be willing and able to bend the rules where appropriate and be creative at meeting varying customer situations while being accountable (at least to some degree) in regard to profitability.

Hence, different characteristics and competencies in people must be sought, different management support systems created, and different metrics evaluated to reward performance and guide the services enterprise. All of this is further complicated because, in many cases, s-businesses still produce and sell products, further adding to the complexity and the challenge.

How to Use This Book

The book is broken down into three intertwined yet separate components:

- *Part One: S-Business—Endless Opportunities.* This succinct, research-based section deals with *strategy*. It paints the big picture and is especially pertinent for business executives examining the strategic potential of s-business.

- *Part Two: A Framework for S-Business Success.* This section on *tactics* provides a practical framework for understanding the six s-business success levers and is appropriate for all services leaders tasked with taking their organizations to the next level of performance.

- *Part Three: Leaping the Chasm.* This section on *transforming* organizations includes the step-by-step, hands-on process of going from "business-as-usual" to "business-as-exceptional." It is must reading for the services change agents tasked with reorienting their organizations toward the s-business approach.

PART ONE

S-Business—Endless Opportunities

Part One gives the reader just enough information about s-business to be dangerous—what it is, what it might do for you, whether it is right for you, and the few, critical differentiators between star performance and the rest of the pack.

Chapter 1 defines s-business, demonstrates its current and potential strategic and financial impact, pinpoints where your organization is currently along the "S-Business Continuum," and helps determine whether s-business is right for your organization.

A succinct Chapter 2 provides a research-based, net-net of the performance of star services businesses followed by the best practices that separate these elite s-businesses from everybody else.

Chapter 1

S-Business Strategy: Going Deep, Going Wide, or Going Nowhere

RESEARCH FACTOID: From a strategic standpoint, almost one-half of the organizations that participated in the global research project (Alexander, 2002) were "Going Nowhere."

PONDER POINT: Most businesses would benefit by making the leap to s-business.

PURPOSE: This chapter will help you determine if s-business is the right business strategy for your organization. The information provided will help you:

- Define your current product-services status on the "S-Business Continuum"
- Analyze the strategic implications of your current position
- Consider the pluses and minuses of making the move to s-business

Although the specific language differs, the best books on business strategy recommend that organization leaders determine which one of the following strategies their businesses should follow: the low-cost provider, market leader, innovator, or niche player. This is sound advice, built around the proven concept that you can't be all things to all people. We are firm believers in this gospel. However, to build upon the premises we propose, it does not go far enough. Organizations must make another strategic choice that impacts their business direction. Organization leaders need to examine their attitudes, actions, and commitment toward their products and services offerings and make a choice regarding which one (products or services) will be emphasized and which will be subservient. As we'll show, a lot is at stake based upon this decision.

We have created a tool, the "S-Business Continuum" (Figure 2) to provide organization leaders a starting point in thinking this through. First we'll help define your organization's current standing by categorizing it along the continuum. Then we'll talk about the strategic pluses and minuses of staying put or making a move up (or down) this product-services scale.

Step 1: Determine Your Organization's Current S-Business Status

The S-Business Continuum classifies an organization based upon its current mix of products and services *and* the business's preference toward one or the other. At the far left of Figure 2 are companies that only sell products and at the far right are organizations that only sell services. In the middle are hybrids

Figure 2: The S-Business Continuum.

Pure Product				Pure Services
1	2	3	4	5

that offer some combination of the two. Using the descriptions listed below, select the one category that best describes the current s-business status of your organization:

1. *Pure product.* We are a product company, period. (We outsource all service or we handle only warranty and product problems with our own people [usually at no charge].)

   The pure product company started with a core product or technology and has never lost this focus. It sees services as inconveniences and prefers not to deal with them at all. It sometimes grudgingly provides them to customers only because it doesn't trust third-party providers to do it correctly—poor service is a blemish to its products.

2. *Services is a cost center.* We aggressively sell products. However, we also provide and charge for "break-fix" services.

   This organization is still definitely product-focused, but because customers want (and will pay for) "manufacturer-authorized" services when there are problems with its products, this type of company has a services department with different rates for defined services offerings.

3. *Services is a profit center, but....* Yes, we sell services and try to make some money on them but our core business and focus are products.

   This type of organization has recognized the revenue and profit contribution that services has to offer and counts on services performance to help accomplish business goals. Usually the services function is well defined, with special services metrics, unique technologies, and established operational procedures. However, even in cases where services is the dominant contributor to revenue and profitability, services is not the fair-haired child. In every situation in which the VP of Services squares off with a VP from the product side, the VP of services loses every time. No matter what the mix of the product/services contribution, it is still a product-centered organization. The thinking, attitudes, and actions all work together to support a product-centric culture.

4. *Services-led*. We are a services-driven business that also sells products.*

Organizations at this point on the continuum "push" services and "pull" along their product offerings. The marketing and selling approach is built around communicating the unique value that their services portfolio brings to bear in meeting customers' needs. Indeed, the organization mindset "thinks services" and the main business goals, rewards, feedback systems, tools, and reinforcements are built around driving services performance first, product performance second.

5. *Pure services*. We provide product support services and/or professional services but no products.

These organizations started as pure services organizations and have stayed that way. There are two distinct types of services organizations that occupy this space: professional services organizations that may offer everything from systems integration to training to management consulting, and independent product support services organizations that provide their customers on-demand response, maintenance, and technical support to maximize the uptime of particular products and applications. Neither of these pure services companies have any desire to build, promote, or sell products.

Step 2: Understand Your Strategic Position

Now let's take a look at your standing from a broad product-services standpoint. Figure 3 shows that 58% (2% "1"s, 8% "2"s, and 48% "3"s) of respondent companies from the s-business research (Alexander, 2002) were classified as product-centered and 42% (20% "4"s and 22% "5"s as s-businesses). The lightning bolt crossing the scale in the figure represents a fundamental divide, a chasm between the product-centered companies on

---

* Note that in this category falls that special type of organization called a *Total Solutions Provider*—an organization that attempts to meet all of a customer's needs around a particular business issue through providing a bundle of professional services, products, and product support services. More about the challenges and opportunities of Total Solutions later.

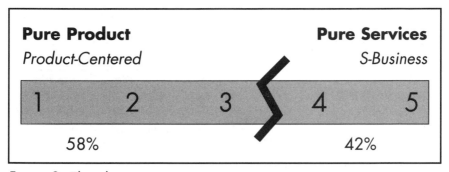

Figure 3: The chasm.

the left and the true services-led s-businesses on the right. No matter what the executives espouse to Wall Street, what the annual reports proclaim, or in actuality what the real business contribution of services are, organizations to the left of the chasm think and breathe products. The s-businesses on the right-hand side have a different culture, one that focuses its value equation squarely around the value of their services offerings.

But what is the business performance consideration for this breakdown? Are there economic benefits to being on the right instead of the left side? Table I shows the comparisons between these two groups on three factors.

Table I compares s-businesses versus product-centered organizations both today (in 2002) and two years hence regarding the services/product percentage of total sales. As expected, the ratio of services to products is much higher for organizations designated as s-business. Both types of organizations anticipated increases in the percentage of services sold, with s-business projecting an increase from 79% to 82% and product-centered businesses predicting an even greater change from 22% today to 30% tomorrow.

Table I also compares the average gross margin of s-businesses versus product-centered companies today (in 2002) and the predicted organizational gross margin objective two years into the future. Regarding the current average gross margin of services sold, s-businesses reported 31% while product-centered organizations stated 29%. There is a statistical difference found

Table I: Business Performance: S-Business Versus Product-Centered Companies

| | Today | | | | Tomorrow | | | |
| | S-Biz | | Product-C | | S-Biz | | Product-C | |
	Svcs	Prds	Svcs	Prds	Svcs	Prds	Svcs	Prds
% Total Sales	79%	21%	22%	78%	82%	18%	30%	70%

| | Today | | | | Tomorrow | | | |
| | S-Biz | | Product-C | | S-Biz | | Product-C | |
	Svcs	Prds	Svcs	Prds	Svcs	Prds	Svcs	Prds
Avg Gross Margin	31%*	11%	29%	28%	37%*	12%	32%	28%

| | Today | | | | Tomorrow | | | |
| | S-Biz | | Product-C | | S-Biz | | Product-C | |
	Svcs	Prds	Svcs	Prds	Svcs	Prds	Svcs	Prds
Annl Growth Rate	22%	7%	16%	11%	25%	8%	22%	16%

* Statistically significant at .05 level.
Source: Alexander, 2002.

in comparing the anticipated services average gross margin of s-businesses with their current profit performance—s-businesses projected major improvements in profitability within a two-year time frame.

Looking at the product average gross margin, product-centered organizations reported a 28% average on products sold today and also felt that their product average gross margin targets in the future would be the same 28%. S-businesses reported that their average gross margins for products was 11% today and would remain flat (12%) two years from then. Product-centered organizations had higher gross profit margins on products than did s-businesses.

Finally, Table I compares the current and the anticipated overall growth rate of the two types of businesses. Services were growing faster than products for both types of organizations currently, with even faster growth projected in the future. Surprisingly, product-centered organizations projected a statis-

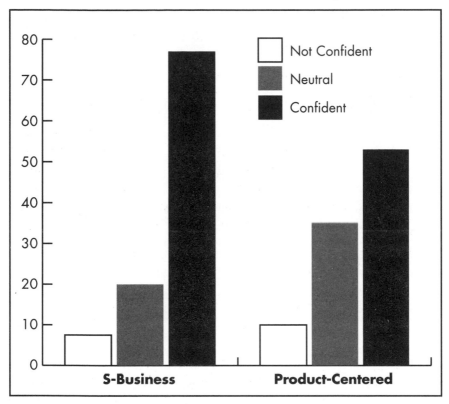

Figure 4: Confidence of s-business and product-centered companies in reaching future goals.

tically valid increase in product growth from 11% to a 16% growth goal in two years. The same was not true for the projected services growth of s-businesses.

Confidence in Reaching Future Goals

How confident these two types of organizations were in reaching their business goals two years into the future is represented in Figure 4. 7% of s-businesses and 11% of product-centered organizations were *not* confident that they would reach their gross margin and growth rate goals two years in the future. 20% of s-businesses and 36% of product-centered companies were neutral on this issue, while 73% of s-businesses and 53% of product-centered companies were confident in reaching these

future performance objectives. Yes, there was a difference—
s-businesses were more confident in their ability to reach their
performance goals two years out.

Performance Highlights

According to the research data, compared to product-centered
organizations s-businesses were:

- Growing their services business faster
- Predicting a significantly higher average gross margin on
  future services sold
- Displaying more confidence in their ability to achieve future
  performance goals

However, compared to s-businesses, product-centered organizations had higher margins on their products and also expected the growth of the product side of their business to increase
significantly in the future.

Step 3: Is S-Business for You?

We know that when it comes to the performance of the services-
side of the enterprise, s-businesses clearly outperform product-
centered organizations. The question then is: Should all
organizations to the left of the chasm make the leap? The
answer is: It depends. For some organizations, crossing the
chasm to s-business is a necessity for survival. For others, the
move is counterproductive. As with many important things in
life, further thought and analysis are required.

The first major consideration relates to the product commoditization factor of the market space your organization is playing in.
The stronger the drive toward commoditization (from the customer's perspective), the more pressure on product gross profit
margins. As a quick review of Table I reveals, s-businesses already
were feeling the effects of commoditization represented by the
significantly lower gross profit margins of products sold compared to services sold. So the stronger the product commoditization trend, the more attractive the move to s-business.

The second major consideration is taking into account the dramatic differences in culture and organizational mindset necessary for effective performance in these two difference worlds. Let's face it, product-minded people think differently than services-oriented folks. Their backgrounds, experiences, and careers have been lived and based upon different business models. Neither thought process is inherently better or worse, they are just quite different. The necessary shift in culture can be made, but it takes considerable effort (Brown, Van Bennekom, Goffin, Hahn, and Alexander, 2001). In fact, our experience in helping clients make this transition from product-centered to services-led is that sometimes the organization needs a major jolt to break away from business-as-usual (more on this topic and the use of a "readiness review" in Chapter 10.)

The third consideration is based upon an organization's specific location on the s-business continuum. Each has different strengths and weaknesses, opportunities and threats. Figure 5 shows that three of the five positions along the path are based upon an overall strategy of "going deep," of being focused upon and being very good at products or being very good at services. Position 4 follows the concept of "going wide" and attempts to maximize revenue potential by offering a full portfolio that is services-led, but also product-rich. Finally, Position 3 on the

Figure 5: Strategic choices.   *Source:* Alexander and Hordes, 2002.

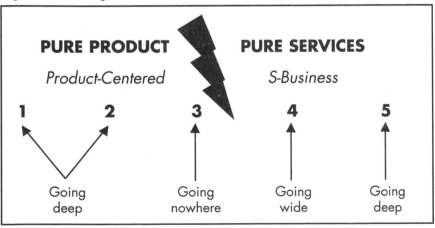

continuum (the position that has the highest proportion of all businesses) has the unenviable stanch of "going nowhere," of not having either the specialization required by depth nor the capabilities demanded of going wide.

Below is a brief description of the three strategies and their s-business implications.

Going Deep

1 (PURE PRODUCT) AND 2 (SERVICES IS A COST CENTER)

The s-business implications are almost identical for organization classified as either a "1" or "2" along the S-Business Continuum, so we've combined them here for simplicity.

Core Competency: Effective organizations at these locations see their main organizational strength as either:

- Product innovation. They strive to lead their market segments by developing and marketing clearly superior (from the customer's perspective) products.
- Low-cost provider. Using their excellence in manufacturing and driven by a philosophy of continuous improvement, these kinds of organizations strive to deliver acceptable product quality at the lowest price and make their money through superior efficiencies.

S-business situation analysis: When you think through the situation strategically, the following strengths and risks/opportunities become evident:

- Strengths: excellent focus, economies of scale
- Risks/opportunities: missing revenue/profit potential of services, vulnerability to total solutions selling

S-business approach: Two options should be considered:

- Continue to ignore services and focus on what you do best.

  Action: Vital to find and secure services partners so as not to be outsold or left out by Total Solutions Providers.
- Explore the s-business opportunity by setting up a separate services organization totally independent of the core product business.

Also note that organizations currently falling in the "services is a cost center" category should consider moving toward the "pure product" category, focusing even more on their product strengths and outsourcing *all* of their basic services needs. This is what focus is all about.

5 (PURE SERVICES)

Although at the other end of the spectrum from Location 1 or 2 organizations, pure services companies share the same basic approach to strategy.

Core competency: High-performance businesses in this location see their main organizational strength as either:

- Services innovation. They strive to lead their market segment by developing and marketing clearly superior (from the customer's perspective) service offerings.
- Low-cost provider. Using their excellence in process and driven by a philosophy of continuous improvement, these organizations strive to deliver acceptable services quality at the lowest price and make their money through superior efficiencies.

S-business situation analysis: For pure services companies, the following strengths and risks/opportunities are evident:

- Strengths: excellent focus, high margins
- Risks/opportunities: missing revenue/profit potential of products, vulnerability to total solutions selling

S-business approach: Two options should be considered:

- Continue to ignore total solutions and focus on what you do best.

Action: Vital to find and secure services partners so as not to be outsold or left out by Total Solutions Providers.

- Explore the total solutions opportunity by assessing existing competence against the requirements for providing total solutions.

Action: Gradually expand your base of capabilities and offerings.

Going Wide

4 (SERVICES-LED)

Core competency: To be effective, these organizations must have strong capabilities across the breadth of their services-product offerings.

- For those Location 4 organizations attempting to deliver total solutions, three more areas of excellence are required:
- Excellent marketplace credibility
- Outstanding account/project/engagement management skills
- A viable partner management system (recruiting/screening/qualifying/developing/nurturing)

S-business situation analysis: For services-led companies, the following strengths and risks/opportunities are evident:

- Strengths: maximum sales potential, opportunity to "own" the account, chance for market
- Risks/opportunities: necessity of balancing product/service conflict
- Requirement of very strong standing in the market
- Ongoing challenge of bias perception
- Very strong prowess a must

S-business approach: Two options should be considered:

- Expand total solutions efforts.

    Action: Place emphasis on creating strong professional services capabilities (especially sales) as this pulls both products and product support services.

- Focus on services.

    Action: Shed product side of things and develop deeper service offerings.

Going Nowhere

3 (SERVICES IS A PROFIT CENTER, BUT…)

Danger Will Robinson!*

This position is the most vulnerable. Neither fish nor fowl,

---

* For those of you too young to be around, too old to remember, or too smart to waste time watching TV, this was the oft-spouted warning of the robot

businesses acting from this business model usually have the following problems:
- They are not maximizing their market potential.
- They suffer from internal friction and turf wars.
- They are prone to inefficiencies

Furthermore, the risk here is magnified because often organizational leaders of Location 3 businesses *talk* and *feel* like they are operating as s-businesses, yet they *think* and *act* like the product executives they truly are.

No matter how successful they are today, in order to prosper in the long-term, organizations in this category must make a move. They should either leap to the right and embrace s-business or fall back toward the left to their origins.

S-business approach:
- Fall back to their origins.
  Action: Spin off the services side of things and focus resources on products.
- Make the leap to s-business.
  Action: Study marketplace needs and internal capabilities, make a plan, and take the jump across the chasm to s-business. Include in the plans a healthy dose of effort to educate everyone involved on the fundamental differences in culture required to fuel the change efforts.

Conclusion

The product-versus-services question is an important element of strategy that needs to be addressed. All organizations can be classified using the S-Business Continuum to determine their current locations with each location having specific strengths and opportunities. Most organizations to the left of the chasm will benefit by making the leap to s-business.

---

tasked with protecting the young Will Robinson from harm in the television series, *Lost in Space.*

Chapter 2

The Best Practices that Separate Star S-Businesses from Everybody Else

RESEARCH FACTOID: According to the global research project results (Alexander, 2002), top-performing s-businesses averaged *61% gross margin* and *30% annual growth rate* on their services offerings.

PONDER POINT: Only a few things separate the good from the great.

PURPOSE: This chapter will demonstrate the performance potential possibilities of an effective s-business. The information provided will help you:

- Benchmark your current services business performance against the stars.
- Learn the fourteen best services-practices (s-practices) of elite s-businesses that separate them from everybody else.

As a part of conducting the fore-mentioned s-business research, fifty-nine core services practices were identified as important to any effective services business. (These will be introduced in Chapters 3 through 8.) Yet, it was hypothesized that organizations that were getting the most impact from their services initiatives were doing certain things quite differently from those organizations obtaining less positive business effects. In order to test these assumptions, respondents were classified into two groups: high performers and low performers. High performers were defined as those organizations that derived at least 25% of their revenue from services and were in the top 25% in achieving gross margins of services offerings.

Thirty-seven organizations met this high-performer criteria and were compared to the 333 low performers* (everybody else).

Geographically, respondents were classified into one of three groupings: U.S., Europe, and the Rest of the World. Statistically there was no difference regarding the proportion of high performers among these three groups. Furthermore, respondents were classified as small (under $50 million U.S.), medium ($50 million to $1 billion U.S.), or large (more than $1 billion U.S.). When it came to size, there was no statistical difference. Of course, as one would anticipate, there were large differences related to business performance.

Table II displays the product/services mix of the high performers compared with that of the low performers. This data supports the trend shown earlier in the report that services are becoming a higher proportion of the product/services mix for all businesses.

Table II also compares high performers to low performers, both today (2002) and in regard to projections two years from

---

* Technically, it is more descriptive to refer to this group as "non-high performers" (although, in fact, many executives would be very pleased with the performance of many organizations that fell into this category), but since this phrase is a little awkward, the term "low performers" is used throughout this section.

Table II: Business Performance:
High-Performers Versus Low Performers

| | Today | | | | Tomorrow | | | |
| | High | | Low | | High | | Low | |
	Svcs	Prds	Svcs	Prds	Svcs	Prds	Svcs	Prds
% Total Sales	79%	21%	42%	58%	81%	19%	48%	52%

| | Today | | | | Tomorrow | | | |
| | High | | Low | | High | | Low | |
	Svcs	Prds	Svcs	Prds	Svcs	Prds	Svcs	Prds
Avg Gross Margin	61%*	14%	26%	22%	59%*	15%	31%	22%

| | Today | | | | Tomorrow | | | |
| | High | | Low | | High | | Low | |
	Svcs	Prds	Svcs	Prds	Svcs	Prds	Svcs	Prds
Annl Growth Rate	30%	5%	17%	10%	29%	7%	23%	14%

* Statistically significant at .05 level.
Source: Alexander, 2002.

then, as to the average gross margins of services sold. On average, the high performers were receiving a 61% gross margin on services compared to a 26% gross margin on services for the low performers. As one would guess, this is statistically significant. High performers said they received a 14% average gross margin on products, with the low performers outperforming them statistically with a 22% average gross margin on products. Furthermore, when comparing the "today" state, high performers anticipated a significantly higher margin on services sold in the future while the low performers did not.

In addition, Table II compares the current and the anticipated overall growth rates of these two groups. Annual growth rate of services was a torrid 30% for high performers, and a respectable 17% for low performers. Regarding products, the high performers stated they had a 5% annual growth rate, while the low performers said they tracked at 10%. Future projections were similar, with none of the comparisons being statistically different.

Although not shown in the table, high performers were statistically more confident than low performers about accomplishing their performance goals two years into the future.

So to net it out, compared to the low performers, high performers were displaying the following characteristics:

- They were enjoying much higher gross margins on their services business
- They were growing their services business faster.
- They were predicting significantly higher average gross margins on future services sold.
- They were displaying more confidence in their ability to achieve future performance goals.

These folks have broken the code. Now we describe the best practices that separated the elite from everybody else.

Best S-Practices Selection Process

Best practices are those select actions done by top performers and not done by average or poor performers. Best practices are organizational differentiators and offer the potential for significant competitive advantage.

Here is the process used to determine the best s-practices:

1. The research to date, combined with expert input and the experience of the researcher, was used to determine fifty-nine potential best practices.
2. Participant organizations were divided into a high-performer group or low-performer group, based on their s-business status and average gross margins for their services offerings (see the first part of this chapter).
3. All practices in which statistical testing revealed a significant difference between the high- and low-performing groups were designated as best s-practices.

Table III: Best S-Practices

1. The overall strategy is based upon "pushing" services and "pulling" products.
2. The top management team includes individuals with services management experience.
3. A services marketing plan is in place.
4. The services value proposition is clearly understood by all stakeholders.
5. "Value-based" pricing is the most common pricing method.
6. The entire sales force has been trained in selling services.
7. Service providers have access to real-time customer information.
8. A common organization-wide project/engagement tracking system is used.
9. Services are *not* organized by geography.
10. Project managers know how to manage project scope.
11. Services providers utilize a common methodology.
12. Services providers demonstrate appropriate selling skills.
13. Services providers possess adequate account management skills.
14. Cost of sales is tracked.

Best S-Practices

The fourteen best s-practices, summarized in Table III, are described in more detail here:

1. *The overall strategy is based upon "pushing" services and "pulling" products.* With rare exceptions, customers see no difference between the product offerings of the top suppliers in any market space. What they value most are the services that maintain product uptime, enhance an application, or (better yet) drive business performance. The smart companies sell the value of these services and then drag the product along with the services sale. Note, however, that the more successful a product- or technology-based organization has been in the past, the more difficult it is for it to

think of the products or technology that made the organization great as commodities. Furthermore, an even more bitter pill to swallow is to consider the always-till-now subservient services as the leader of the pack. This is a considerable shift of mind for individuals to accept and requires the organization to make a major cultural adaptation over time. Yet, this best s-practice is the heart of s-business, and the main difference between those listed as 3's and 4's on the S-Business Continuum mentioned in Chapter 1.

2. *The top management team includes individuals with services management experience.* Let's face it, product folks think (and act) differently than services people—they have different ways of viewing the business, different ways of measuring success, different ways of marketing, selling, and so on. If you are going to be services-driven, then there needs to be services horsepower on the bridge to help chart a new business heading. This brings up an interesting challenge, though. Till now, there has been very little demand for services executives (except of course in pure services organizations), and hence few people from the services discipline hold the most senior executive positions within most companies. With this very limited demand, few services managers have had the exposure, experience, and/or the executive education opportunities often afforded the best and the brightest from other disciplines. Therefore, at a time when services executives are most needed, few are ready to take on the role.

3. *A services marketing plan is in place.* Chapter 4 will get into more detail about this, but there are fundamental differences between products and services, and trying to market (and sell) services the same way products are sold is a recipe for disaster. Importantly, since services are the lead for s-businesses, the services marketing plan becomes the driver for all marketing messages. Services must be an integral part of the overall business plan and not just a few paragraphs in the operations or product marketing section.

4. *The services value proposition is understood clearly by all stakeholders.* Want to win an easy bet? Tell *any* CEO that the people of his or her organization do not understand the company's value proposition. When he/she violently disagrees with your statement, walk him/her out to the receptionist and ask the question "What value does our company's offerings give to our customers?" After a few minutes of off-track comments, a red-faced CEO will concede your wager. Sad as this may seem, our unofficial estimate is that this is the case in at least eight of ten organizations. Now think about this scenario from a services perspective, and a two-fold marketing challenge appears. Outside, long-standing customers that often know your organization for the products it sells have to be educated, sold, and convinced about the value of your services and your capabilities in delivering them. Not always an easy task. Furthermore, inside the organization, everyone needs to learn the significance of services to organization success and to be able to articulate these benefits. Again, this is a challenge of (sometimes) large proportions, but one that must be met.

5. *"Value-based" pricing is the most common pricing method.* Those who have been around services a while know there are a number of ways to price them: time and materials, percentage of list (specifically for product support services), cost-plus, competitive match, and a number of hybrids. However, the common element of the above is their tendency to commoditize services. When the customer sees services and services providers as relatively equal, traditional pricing methods put the focus on buying services competitively (by the pound), and of course the conversation then focuses on lowering the price. However, a noticeable exception to the above pricing options is that the top-performing services businesses use value-based pricing significantly more often than the not-so-high-performing services businesses. Value-based pricing of course requires a high skill level for those involved in business development: being able to clearly

understand and articulate the potential business impact of solving a problem or seizing an opportunity, getting a prospect to also see this performance potential and quantify it in his/her terms, and then coming up with a project-based price that seems fair to the prospect as well as potentially very profitable to the services organization. Clients will tell you that they prefer this method as it focuses on what is most important to them, it adds clarity by requiring buyers and sellers to hammer out and define clear objectives and quantifiable results, and it is simple—it results in one price. There is a certain tranquility about not having to constantly worry about the meter running.

6. *The entire sales force has been trained in selling services.* As will be noted throughout this book, selling skills are key differentiators of star versus non-star services organizations, and, as such, everyone in a business development role needs to have the appropriate knowledge, skills, and indeed the appropriate mindset to sell services. Off-the-shelf sales training programs can provide basic skills, but they are based upon an old product paradigm and their value is quickly diluted when faced with the unique challenges of selling services in a complex, multi-level solution sale. Hence, a differentiating characteristic of top-performing companies in the services area is their ongoing commitment to providing quality *services-specific* training to everyone involved in the selling process.

7. *Services providers have access to real-time customer information.* Whether we are talking about management consultants, customer engineers, or service technicians, the ability to get the right information the right way, anywhere, anytime is an important component in performance. It is directly related to real-time customer satisfaction as well as to compressing services cycle time. For years, this concept of always being accessible to customers was merely a dream or in place only in rare situations. No more. The technology is available, the cost is affordable, and it works.

8. *A common organization-wide project/engagement tracking system is used.* *Common* is the important adjective in this sentence. Without common reports, how can the services executive ever analyze strengths and weaknesses, identify priority opportunities, or compare performance across services lines, offerings, marketplaces, and services providers? Furthermore, without this approach, Best Practices 7 above can never be realized either. Whether supported by a CRM *(customer relationship management)*, separate PSA *(professional services automation)* software, or an Excel spreadsheet, the best organizations track projects, engagements, and all contacts with customer organizations in the same way. Whether one is a sales person or services provider, in Hong Kong or in Houston, everyone uses one system, in one way.

9. *Services are not organized by geography.* Top-performing services businesses were significantly less likely to be organized by geography, preferring other means such as by industry or by account. Depending on the "mission-criticality" of your services, the sophistication of your services offerings, the need for "feet on the street" (versus remote service or self-service), the type of clients you serve, and where services are needed, this can be a very challenging practice to implement. However, the data shows that if your organization is currently organized geographically, it is definitely worth considering a change through the redeploying of existing personnel, rethinking deployment options, reformatting (and simplifying) service offerings, adding appropriately skilled people, or the building of alliances.

10. *Project managers know how to manage project scope.* "Scope creep" has long been the bane of project managers whatever the industry. A client request just slightly beyond the specifications of the project, a service provider trying to deliver "knock the socks off service" when it is uncalled for, performance standards (and rewards) tilted toward keeping the customer happy no matter how unreasonable his or her requests, or services executives too willing to intervene when

a client calls to complain—are the result of project managers not having either the understanding of the negative impact of scope creep, the knowledge or skills to deal with it effectively, or the motivation to address the problem due to management non-support.

11. *Services providers utilize a common methodology.* Again the word *common* pops up since high-performing organizations make sure that services delivery follows a common approach no matter when, where, or what types of services are being delivered. Of course each situation has some difference that must be adjusted for, but 80% to 95% of the delivery process should be the same for any project or engagement regardless of type of customer, industry, or location.

12. *Services providers demonstrate appropriate selling skills.* In most services organizations, service providers outnumber their business development colleagues on an order 5:1 to 20:1 or more. Furthermore, these folks are walking the customer's halls and rubbing shoulders with the frontline folks often on a daily basis. Who better knows the company's customers, their issues, and their needs? Who in the services organization has more respect and trust? In a highly competitive time, where better to get new business (fast and easy) than by growing customer share? We will wager that in organizations that have not already done so, business can be increased 20% within 90 days through the following steps:

- Communicating to employees the importance of service providers getting new business
- Providing them with business development objectives and enticing incentives for performance
- Giving them quality training and supportive tools to do the job

This is easy to do, can be done quickly, and generates immediate results.

13. *Services providers possess adequate account management skills.* This is just one level up from Best Practice 12. It means that

not only do services providers have a clear role in business development, they also assume some level of responsibility for and the knowledge and skills required in managing and growing accounts.

14. *Cost of sales is tracked.* An earlier study conducted by one of the authors (Alexander, 2000) showed that many services organizations (in this case specifically professional services organizations) didn't know their cost of sales. The s-business study confirmed what that implied: Tracking cost of sales is an important activity to be built into the services performance system. Cost of sales (mainly the opportunity time of those involved on the selling team) is directly related to selling cycle time, as the longer it takes to get (or not get) a sale, the more time, and hence the more cost, is involved. As will be pointed out later in the book, the major contributors to high cost of sales are not defining what ideal business looks like, and not teaching those involved in the business development process how to use key events in the selling process to get either fast "nos" or fast "yeses."

Conclusion

Compared to the low performers, high performers are doing the following:

- Enjoying much higher profits on their services business
- Growing their services business faster
- Predicting significantly higher average gross margins on future services sold
- Displaying more confidence in their ability to achieve future performance goals

For those organizations committed to being high-performance, services-driven s-businesses, the fourteen best s-practices are the actions that, if implemented, one could expect to have a direct effect on business profitability and the possibility of helping create competitive advantage in the marketplace.

PART TWO

A Framework for
S-Business Success

Part Two is for the s-business leader looking for a no-nonsense framework for improving services performance. No matter the current organization strategy, nor the maturity of your services business, all services leaders will benefit from this section. Key success levers are introduced, tools are provided, areas to exploit are shown, and core practices are described that can have immediate impact.

Figure 6 shows our six-lever s-business performance model that serves as a framework for determining performance opportunities. Inside each lever are the enablers necessary for optimum results. Starting with Chapter 3 (strategy) and continuing through Chapter 8 (talent), each chapter addresses each of the performance levers more in depth.

Strategy	**Marketing**	**Selling**
Value proposition Services offerings Drivers Differentiators Critical metrics	Market message Brand building Pricing Services portfolio management	Qualifying process Committing process
Delivery	**Operations**	**Talent**
Engagement model Services execution	Leverage model Knowledge management Service quality	Recruiting Hiring Developing Retaining

Figure 6: The six s-business success levers.

Chapter 3

S-Business Strategy: Four Paths to Greatness

RESEARCH FACTOID: Two-thirds of services organization leaders participating in the global research project (Alexander, 2002) felt that their services strategy was only partially effective.

PONDER POINT: No matter how talented your organization, if you don't have the right strategy you'll always suffer spotty customer satisfaction, fight problems of morale, and have to live with subpar performance.

PURPOSE: This chapter will help you improve your s-business strategy by helping you to do the following:

- Think about strategy starting with what the customer values and how the customer perceives your services organization
- Learn the differences among the four types of services providers

- Understand the core elements and key enablers of each of the four services strategies
- Align your services strategy to your overall business strategy

Chapter 1 looked at strategy from the view of an airliner flying at 40,000 feet. It was aimed at helping you to determine which one of the five potential strategic points on the S-Business Continuum is most reflective today of your overall business and most appropriate tomorrow based upon your existing product-services portfolio and your organization's product-services mindset. Chapter 3 brings the vantage point down to crop duster level, helping you determine and refine the most appropriate services strategy for your organization. First the enablers of the services strategy success lever are explained. Next the four types of services providers are defined from the customer point of view. Then, the four services strategies are explained relative to the four types of services providers, followed by an analysis of how appropriately they align with the overall business strategy.

Figure 7 shows the enablers that are essential components of the services strategy. Your *value proposition* explains how you intend to benefit targeted customers. Your *services offerings* target the types of services most appropriate for your strategy. *Drivers* are what are vital to your strategic success. *Differentiators*

Figure 7: The strategy success lever.

Strategy

Value proposition
Services offerings
Drivers
Differentiators
Critical metrics

are what make you different and better than your competitors. *Critical metrics* are the few performance measures most important to your strategy. Each of these enablers will be talked about in more detail later in the chapter.

A Brief Word About Strategy

Business strategy has been looked at in many ways for many years in many books devoted to the subject. Although several factors influence strategic decisions, for the most part we will try and focus on the ones unique and/or vital to services businesses. For example, segmentation is a core element of any strategy, but a topic that we will touch on only briefly because it is not unique to services.

Our point of view is that the simplest and most powerful way to analyze services strategy is by emphasizing two factors: the *importance* of your portfolio of services offerings to the customer and the *uniqueness* of your offerings in the marketplace. This outside-in approach forces an ongoing reality check and helps to minimize the myopia that often seems to set in when strategic planners and executives develop strategy without a constant and healthy dose of customer reality. As an aside, we will wager that *all* of your main customers would have no trouble in quickly placing you and your main competitors in one of the strategy quadrants about to be described. So to start with, it makes sense to ground our thinking in how customers view and classify services providers.

The Four Types of Services Providers

Figure 8 shows services providers classified by services importance and services uniqueness. The names we've chosen to represent these classifications help to quickly describe who they are: Vendors, Specialists, Total Solutions Providers, and Game Changers.

Which quadrant a customer places you in has a direct relationship to how you will be viewed, how much time will be

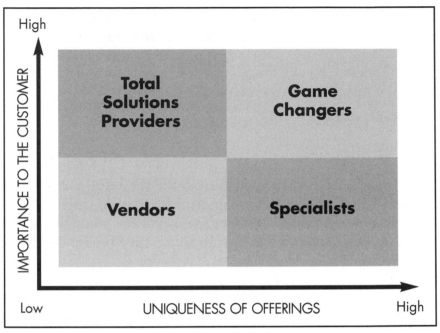

Figure 8: The four types of service providers.

spent on you, how high up in the organization your offerings will be considered, and how much money you will be allowed to make. Obviously, this categorization is an important one for your services organization. Four elements—value potential, expectations, who buys, and buying strategy—help to shape the customer's decision.

Value Potential

At its most basic level, value is defined as benefits minus cost.

Figure 9 displays the value potential for each type of services provider from the customers' eyes. Customers see little value in the offerings of Vendors because they regard them as being of low importance and low uniqueness. Specialists however, provide services that are unique—usually not big-ticket items, but special services that are required nonetheless. Hence, the value potential to customers is medium. Total Solutions Providers offer big-dollar, high-profile services (usually bundled with products), yet there are competitors that (customers feel) can do the same thing equally as

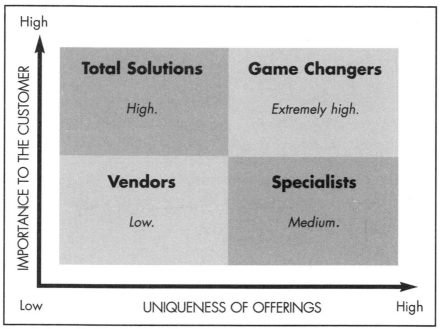

Figure 9: Value potential.

well. Therefore, the services are not unique, but important nonetheless, and are thus of high potential value to customers. Game Changers are the few services providers possessing highly unique offerings that are mission-critical to customers. The potential value of this relationship is extremely high to customers as successful implementation will directly impact critical business issues.

Expectations

The customer expectations we are interested in are the ones they find most important—the ones customers will pay for.

Because of their low potential value, customers buying offerings from Vendors don't want to spend much time or energy in the purchasing process—all they want are offerings of *acceptable* quality, ones that are easy to buy, at low prices. All things being seen as equal, the lowest price always wins.

Because Specialists have unique capabilities, customers expect best-in-class services from them. Since there are very few providers (and sometimes only one) of these services, customers

Figure 10: Customer expectations.

are always wary of being taken advantage of. Customers don't mind paying a premium for these services (they have to have them), but are always concerned about not having the services available when they need them. Hence, they are always looking for other options to meet their specific needs.

When buying from a Total Solutions Provider, the purchase is high-visibility (and high-risk to the backers of the selected services provider). As shown in Figure 10, first on the list of expectations is reliability—the sign of assurance that the services provider can do what it says it will do. Next, customers want one-stop shopping as many big complex purchases involve many suppliers, and they want one and only one organization to act as the agent to address their initiatives. Finally, of course customers want the solutions to work. However (although they will seldom admit it), they are not looking for the very best answers; otherwise, they would have hand-picked the team of diverse specialists required to do the job.

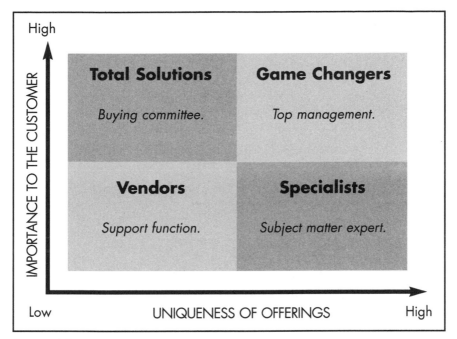

Figure 11: Buyers.

Customers expect only one thing from Game Changers—innovative answers that positively impact business performance.

Who Buys

Although there may be influencers, sponsors, and users of services offerings, there is only one person (or group) tasked with making the actual purchase.

Purchasing from Vendors is usually delegated to a junior member of a support function such as purchasing. Since the services offerings of Vendors aren't seen as important, it makes sense to give the responsibility to a lower-level person.

The buyers of Specialist offerings are often subject matter experts who understand the intricacies and sophistication of these offerings and act to help determine requirements and rate performance.

As shown in Figure 11, because of the size of the sale, the complexity of its implementation, or the breadth of functions its

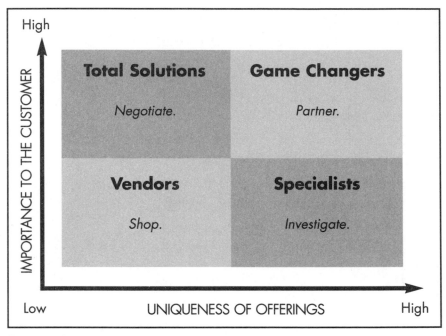

Figure 12: Buying strategy.

application will impact, a buying committee is the standard purchasing mechanism for purchasing Total Solutions. Usually headed by a department senior manager, the team is usually composed of cross-functional professionals, and sponsored by an executive.

The buyers of the services of Game Changers can only be top management because only this group is charged with strategic decisions. In most cases, this responsibility falls to the CEO.

Buying Strategy

The buying strategy (Figure 12) is the organization's philosophy on its approach to purchasing.

When buying from Vendors, the buying strategy is always to shop around for the best deal. An important consideration here, though, is that not much time will be spent. Hence, a deal that looks good after only two or three comparisons may be made so as to save the time that would be required for a thorough search.

When purchasing from Specialists, the buying strategy is to continually investigate other potential suppliers and substitute services.

When considering purchasing from Total Solutions Providers, there are always at least two or three services businesses that customers feel can adequately do the job. Since there are only minor areas of uniqueness, once the short list is finalized, the buying strategy is to negotiate—to seek better terms, to get a few more services tossed in, to get the cost lowered a bit.

When the critical business issues of the organization are at stake, customers will aggressively try to partner with those they see as Game Changers since they realize that organizations with these capabilities are few and far between. They will pay just about anything (within reason) to get the job done "world class."

Summary of Services Providers

The list below summarizes these key elements by each type of services provider:

- Vendors
  - Low importance and low uniqueness
  - Value potential: low
  - Customer expectations: meet my specifications; make it easy to for me to buy; give me the lowest price
  - Buyers: support functions (such as purchasing)
  - Buying strategy: shop
- Specialists
  - Low importance and high uniqueness
  - Value potential: medium
  - Customer expectations: provide best-of-class services; give me options; don't take advantage of me
  - Buyers: subject matter experts
  - Buying strategy: investigate
- Total Solutions Providers
  - High importance and low uniqueness

- Value potential: high
- Customer expectations: reliability, one-stop shopping, acceptable solution
- Buyers: buying committee with senior management sponsors
- Buying strategy: negotiate
- Game Changers
  - High importance and high uniqueness
  - Value potential: extremely high
  - Customer expectations: improved business performance through innovation
  - Buyers: top management
  - Buying strategy: partner

Out of One Box and Into Another

That's it...like it or not, all of your customers have put you in one of the four boxes along with your competitors. Do customers see you where you think you are? Sadly, often they do not. Unfairly pegged? Want to make a move? All is not lost! You can reinvent yourself. You can change their perceptions over time through smart marketing, focused communications, and innovative communication strategies that "tell your story" from a new and fresh perspective. It is a slow and deliberate process, but doable nonetheless. Chapter 4 will provide the tools necessary for this migration.

However, see the sidebar "Oh, no. We're a Vendor!" for a quick example of what to do if the senior management team cries out in unison, " But I don't want to be a vendor!"

The Four Services Strategies

We have seen how customers view services providers and that they think and act quite differently in addressing each type. The smart services executive realizes that the most successful services strategy is the one that best aligns with how the marketplace sees you. There is a corresponding services strategy appropriate for

"Oh, no. We're a Vendor!"

If you are placed in the Vendor box (rightly or wrongly) and want to make a move, your best bet is trying for the Specialist position. This has the least risk and is the most plausible change from the customers' perspective. For the next two to three years, add new capabilities in a specialty area and plow the profits of your services business into a re-positioning and re-branding campaign. Start by conducting some serious market research with some serious dollars behind it to investigate the top competitors who play in the specialty box you wish to occupy. Find out what services they offer, how they sell, how they price, and how they deliver. Discover what customers like and dislike about them and where the opportunities lie. Bring in outside experts to learn their thinking on the targeted space today and the trends for tomorrow. Find your niche and start to break that box wide open. Next, incubate a few new specialty services and make a big play with them to attract customers on a "pilot" basis. With some learning and success behind you, now it is time to start the promotional efforts. Hire public relations (PR) support and take your successes and tout them with strong testimonials from satisfied customers in the appropriate industry rags. Make it an organizational issue to write (and publish) white papers and articles. Sponsor selected conferences or symposia and make sure that you (and/or your customers) demonstrate their expertise and tell your story to the right people. Use some of the marketing approaches discussed in Chapter 4 to develop the new market message and communicate it both outside and inside your organization. Soon you will be seen as a Specialist with all the benefits and minuses that accompany that services provider position.

each of the four types of services providers. Starting from the customer perspectives outlined above, each strategy has distinct pluses and minuses, yet one and only one services strategy is appropriate for each kind of provider. Trying to be all things to all people leads to confusion, poor performance, and gross inefficiency.

It is important to note that any of these strategies, appropriately implemented, can lead to prosperity, even great success. The services organizations that will be the most successful will be the ones that most align their services strategy with the issues, wants, needs, and expectations of their customers.

The Lean and Mean strategy (Figure 13) is appropriate for Vendors. No matter what your capabilities, how superior your services are over the competition, or what your promotional literature says, if the customer pegs you as a Vendor you better act like a Vendor if you wish to survive. Therefore, since customers see your offerings as generic, you might as well accept that fact

Figure 13: The four services strategies.

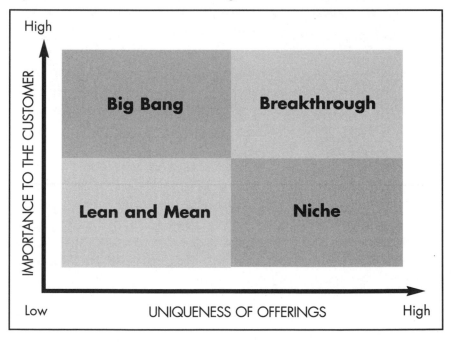

and do the specific things necessary for implementing this particular strategy. Examples of services businesses following the Lean and Mean strategy include Unysis and the large Indian information technology (IT) company, Tata.

The Niche strategy is appropriate when you are seen by your customers as a Specialist—a mile deep in whatever your particular expertise happens to be. The flip side is that they don't see you as playing in other areas and will discount you if you try to expand beyond your expert core. Because services businesses employing a Niche strategy are highly specialized and often smaller firms, there is a good chance you may not have heard of those outside your industry. For example, Datatel targets its IT professional services solely in the higher education marketplace, and PRTM focuses almost entirely on supply chain management.

The Big Bang strategy is appropriate for the Total Solutions Provider, when an organization's services are basically generic in the customer's eyes, yet the services are important to the buying organization due to their overall cost or their potential impact. This is the realm of the very big players such as IBM and Accenture.

Finally, a Breakthrough strategy is appropriate for Game Changers, when your organization's services are very unique and address the mission-critical issues of customers. Here customers will gladly treat you as a partner since you have something very important that they want. Good examples here would be the strategy firms Boston Consulting Group and Marakon.

Value Proposition
The value proposition (Figure 14) is your benefit communication vehicle. It is what you need to be known for to be successful.

Services companies following a Lean and Mean strategy know they are in the commodities business. Customers are *always* putting pressure on price, so to make money services providers pursuing a Lean and Mean Strategy must be the low-cost provider. The low-cost leader can do well in this category, the

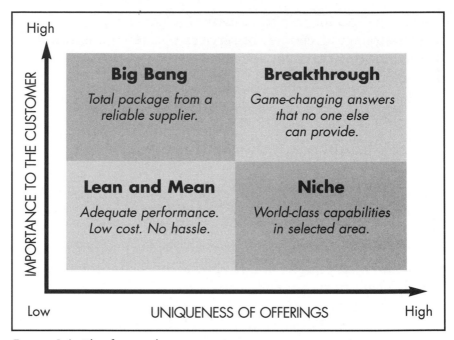

Figure 14: The four value propositions.

second best in cost can eke out a living, while all others are doomed to a slow (and probably painful) death.

The value proposition of the Niche services provider is one built upon world-class capabilities in a narrow specialty. As the issues are often complex and involve many players, the appropriate value proposition for a Total Solutions Provider trying to implement a Big Bang strategy is one that provides a totally hassle-free package. The appropriate value proposition of the Breakthrough strategy must be dramatic and attempt to change the game through capabilities that only this service provider possesses.

Services Offerings

One of the biggest services strategy pitfalls is that most organizations don't take the trouble to define and classify their offerings precisely enough. They try to use the same basic techniques for services that often differ dramatically in their characteristics. More importantly, organizations often use the

Product support	Professional services	Total solutions
Maintenance contracts	Needs analysis	ERP
On-site servicing	Strategy formulation	CRM
Installation	System integration	BPO
Remote monitoring	Readiness reviews	Change
Help desk	System redesign	management
		Six sigma

Figure 15: The three types of services offerings.

same approaches for services that customers see and understand completely differently. The outcome is misplaced resources, customer confusion, and waste. To further emphasize the importance of clearly addressing the issue of the types of services offerings is the confusion regarding the terms used in the services industry. Say "professional services" to one individual and a vision of an impeccably clad suave-looking person addressing a corporate board comes to mind. Another individual hearing the professional services term may think of putting ties on their services technicians. Clearly, some definition is in order. Figure 15 shows our classification for your consideration.

Product support services are exactly what the name implies, services designed to make the product and the application and processes that it is a part of perform better. Hence these services typically try to maximize uptime and increase productivity. Product installation, on-going maintenance, on-site services, and remote monitoring are all typical product support service offerings, often put into services contracts.

Professional services are knowledge-based offerings not tied to a particular product. Most are geared toward issues requiring special intellect. Examples of services offerings typically called *professional services* include: assessments, readiness reviews, strategy consulting, technology consulting, systems integration, project management, network/system design, process engineering, and so on. Some organizations prefer to think of professional services as "pre-sale" (occurring before the purchase of the product) and product support services as "post-sale" (occurring after the sale). However, this is not always the case.

Total Solutions are a blend of professional services, product support services, and products that bundle a variety of offerings to meet the customer's full life cycle of needs surrounding a particular issue. Business Process Outsourcing (BPO), Enterprise Resource Planning (ERP), Customer Relationship Management (CRM), Change Management, and Six Sigma are good examples as they are usually large-scale, complex, and cross the entire organization and sometimes the entire enterprise.

Naturally the type of services offering most appropriate for your services organization to offer depends your strategy and what your targeted customers want, expect, and will pay for. Each of the four strategies has one type of offering that best suits it.

As shown in Figure 16, players in the Lean and Mean zone have the potential to effectively offer product support services and/or professional services. The only requirement is that either grouping of services be seen as a commodity and not extremely important to the customer. For example, on-going technical training might be a product support services offering appropriate for a vendor to sell and deliver. Conducting a certification audit on a non-vital process would be a representative professional service appropriate for this category.

Niche strategists can also offer product support and/or professional services if the services are seen by the customer as unique and low to moderately important to the customer's business. An example professional services offering in this strategic quadrant could be building selling services capabilities. A services contract on a Niche product could be an example of an appropriate product support services offering.

The Total Solutions Providers that try to implement a Big Bang strategy market, sell, and deliver a mix of services and products. Trying to sell bits and pieces is not appropriate as it is

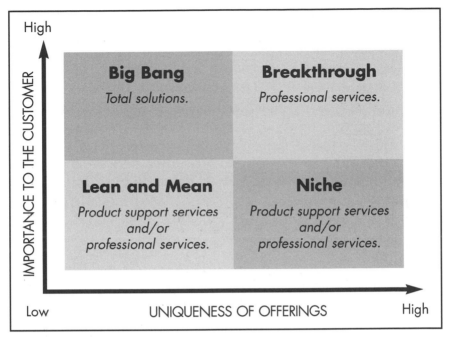

Figure 16: Types of services offerings.

counter to the focus. An example of a Total Solutions offering could be CRM or Six Sigma.

Finally, Game Changers attempting to realize a Breakthrough strategy must keep their eye on those professional services that can have the most impact—ones highly important to customers and ones in which their expertise is highly unique. An example professional services offering falling within this strategy might be leading the transition from a product-centered company to a services-led, s-business.

Drivers

Drivers (Figure 17) are the core attitudes you need for success in the services business realm.

Efficiency is the driver mantra of the Lean and Mean strategy. Such Vendors are always looking to do things easier, faster, cheaper. Their internal philosophy is something like this: Don't make a personal visit if a telephone conversation will do. Don't

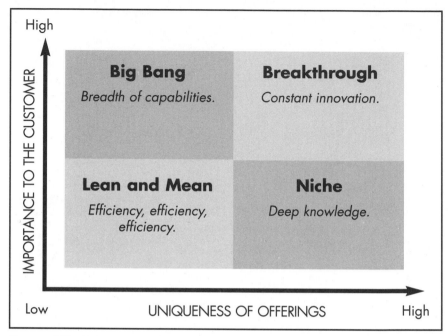

Figure 17: Drivers.

touch the phone if e-mail can handle things. Don't touch the keypad if the customer can use the Web.

To maintain their leadership positions, Specialists that follow the Niche strategy strive to continue to deepen their already vast knowledge and expertise of their selected specialties. Total Solutions Providers following the Big Bang strategy continually expand the breadth of offerings in terms of building, buying, or partnering. The driver of the Breakthrough strategy is innovation; Game Changers must be constantly on the cutting edge, promoting new and dramatically better offerings.

Differentiators

Differentiators (Figure 18) are the core competencies most appropriate for supporting your strategy.

Differentiators for a Lean and Mean strategy must support efforts to be the low-cost provider. Two of the most effective options are being very good at streamlining and optimizing core

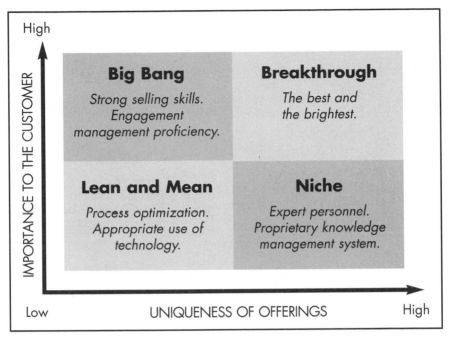

Figure 18: Differentiators.

processes and adopting appropriate technology to automate and simplify processes and tasks.

Differentiators for the Niche strategy start with the highly specialized expertise of personnel coupled with a strong proprietary knowledge management system that captures and distributes the critical information that makes a company different from its competitors—such companies are the keepers of the benchmarks and practices for their industries.

Big Bang strategy differentiators include high-level selling skills (often internally called *senior executive client development capabilities*), which are a must for success. Furthermore, strong engagement management capabilities that set and manage customer and partner expectations and deliver results on time, up to quality, and within budget are absolutes for making money.

The most important breakthrough strategy differentiator is the extraordinary talents and skills of the Game Changer's professionals, who should be made up of only A players.

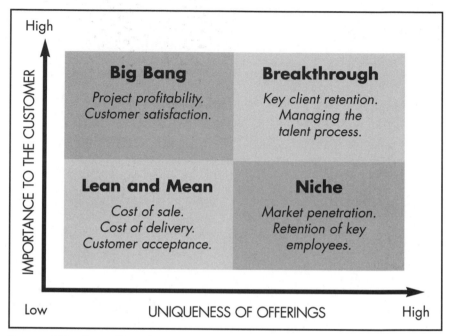

Figure 19: Critical metrics.

Critical Metrics

Critical metrics (Figure 19) are the means by which success is measured.

Three of the main metrics that Lean and Mean organizations should track are cost of sale, cost of delivery, and customer acceptance. The concept of "customer acceptance" is a vital one to grasp, especially since it flies in the face of all the hoopla over customer satisfaction of the last two decades. If you are implementing a Lean and Mean strategy, approaches that "under-promise and over-deliver" or "knock their socks off" are the kiss of death. Customers will gladly take additional services, but they won't pay for them. The secret of customer acceptance is to clearly define exact expectations (what customers will pay for) and deliver exactly that—no more and no less. Deliver less and you have an unsatisfied customer. Deliver more and you have wasted resources and made a customer wonder why you are so foolish as to give away services in a low-cost game.

When pursuing a Niche strategy, your market is limited, so a critical metric is market penetration of all potential customers. Furthermore, retention of key employees is a must as they carry around your intellectual capital between their ears.

The Big Bang strategy is implemented by a series of big projects. Hence, project profitability is a key indicator of success coupled with satisfied customer ratings.

Finally, the Breakthrough strategy is best measured by key client retention, and your ability to manage the talent process: finding, recruiting, hiring, developing, and retaining star performers.

To summarize the four services strategies:

- Lean and Mean
  - Type of services provider: Vendor
  - Value proposition: adequate performance, low cost, no hassle
  - Services offerings: product support services and/or professional services
  - Drivers: efficiency, efficiency, efficiency
  - Differentiators: process optimization, appropriate use of technology
  - Organization: geographic
  - Critical metrics: cost of sale, cost of delivery, customer acceptance
- Niche
  - Type of services provider: Specialist
  - Value proposition: world-class capabilities in selected area
  - Services offerings: product support services and/or professional services
  - Driver: deep knowledge of select topic or field
  - Differentiators: expertise of personnel, proprietary knowledge management system
  - Organization: industry.
  - Critical metrics: market penetration, retention of key employees

- Big Bang
  - Type of services provider: Total Solutions (or Select Providers) Provider
  - Value proposition: total package from a reliable supplier
  - Services offerings: Total Solutions
  - Driver: breadth of offerings
  - Differentiators: high-level selling skills, engagement management competency
  - Organization: account
  - Critical Metrics: project profitability, customer satisfaction
- Breakthrough
  - Type of services provider: Game Changer
  - Value proposition: game-changing solutions that no one else can provide
  - Services offerings: professional services
  - Driver: constant innovation
  - Differentiator: the best and the brightest in the field
  - Organization: account
  - Critical metrics: key client retention; managing the talent process

Aligning the Services Strategy with the Business Strategy

So far we've shown that customers treat different types of services providers quite differently, and that there are four specific services strategies, each one best aligning to a specific services provider type. At this point, another alignment issue must be considered: the alignment of the services strategy with the overall business strategy. For this, we revisit the S-Business Continuum introduced in Chapter 1 and discuss the compatibility of each of the four services strategies with each of the five points on that continuum.

If you are a pure services organization (Point 5 on the S-Business Continuum) then your services strategy *is* the business strategy. Any of the four services strategies are viable options.

If your organization is services-driven and you push services and pull products (Point 4), any of the four services strategies are also relevant possibilities. This is because services are the primary value contributors, with products being seen as low-value elements of the services-led solution.

If your services organization is a profit center in a product-dominated organization (Point 3), as long as it doesn't interfere (or compete) with the product side of the house, Lean and Mean, Niche, and Big Bang are all possible services strategies. However, the Breakthrough services strategy is not an option. Even if your organization sells breakthrough products, it won't tolerate or even consider breakthrough services as that would shift the "balance of power" from products to services, which would be culturally unacceptable.

If services are a cost center (Points 1 or 2), your choice of services strategy has already been made for you—Lean and Mean. Since your company's attempts to add value to its customers are all based upon its products, services are viewed by both the company and its customer as extensions of the products. Hence, a customer will accept new services, but never pay for them. So the services executive needs to limit the amount of services and deliver them as efficiently and as cost-effectively as possible. Furthermore, how the Lean and Mean strategy is implemented in cost-center organizations is a little different than what was described above. For cost-center services organizations, see the sidebar "But What If Services Is a Cost Center."

Conclusion

Customers classify all services providers into one of four types, like it or not. To run a successful company, the services executive must adopt one, and only one, services strategy that aligns with the customers' viewpoint and is compatible with the overall business strategy.

But What If Services Is a Cost Center?

The only purpose of services organizations that are cost centers is to support the product. Therefore, only the Lean and Mean strategy is appropriate since the product is intended to be the sole value contributor. However, some of the elements of the Lean and Mean strategy need to be adjusted to meet different situations. Below are key considerations for both the Vendor type and the Lean and Mean services strategy:

Low importance and low uniqueness

Value potential: very low

Customer expectations: a product that works

Buyers: maintenance managers

Buying strategy: give it to me

Type of services provider: Vendor

Market message: none—trying to be invisible

Mission: "Efficient, fast service when you need it"

Focus: lower cost, lower cost, lower cost

Differentiators: not an issue.

Critical metrics: cost of delivery, customer acceptance

Chapter 4

S-Business Marketing: Making the Strategy Come Alive

RESEARCH FACTOID: The global research project (Alexander, 2002) revealed that in 28% of organizations, *nobody* was in charge of services marketing.

PONDER POINT: Marketing services *inside* the organization are just as important as marketing services *outside* the organization.

PURPOSE: This chapter will help you keep the services marketing focus you need to make the services strategy come alive. You will learn how to:

- Create a market message consistent with the services strategic value proposition
- Build the brand to create credibility
- Establish appropriate services offerings
- Define an appropriate pricing model

In addition, you will learn to:
- Manage the ongoing erosion of existing services lines
- Effectively introduce new services offerings
- Implement core and best services marketing practices
- Live within a framework of services marketing principles

For every services organization, the ability to maintain focus in the marketplace is a mandatory imperative for both effective performance today and building competitive advantage in the future. Focus is important to all businesses, but it's vital to services organizations because the "means of production" occur between the ears of a finite group of people. Thus, using valuable resources (personnel) on non-core activities is wasted opportunity. In fact, the s-business research study (Alexander, 2002) showed that practices that create consistent focus are important differentiators between top-performing services organizations and their lower-performing counterparts. Creating and keeping this focus is a core element of services marketing's mission. (Alexander and Hordes, 2002)

The marketing enablers (Figure 20) of market message, brand building, pricing, and portfolio management will be examined shortly, but first we turn to a brief discussion on the unique challenges of services marketing.

Figure 20: The marketing success lever.

Marketing

Market message
Brand building
Pricing
Services portfolio management

The Services Marketing Challenge

In many ways, most businesses today are doing a lousy job of marketing. The cost of capturing customers continues to rise as buying processes become more complex and selling cycles lengthen. At the same time, customer loyalty is eroding—on average a US-based company loses half of its customers in five years (Reichheld, 1996). Forced by the changing expectations of customers and competitive posturing, most companies expect that one-third of their sales over the next three to five years will come from new products/services and line extensions. Yet, one-half of new offerings launched fail to meet business goals (Cespedes, 1994) and two-thirds of new offerings ideas never achieve market success (Donath, 1992). *So currently about 50 to 65 cents out of every marketing dollar invested in new offerings is wasted.*

The above marketing challenges are formidable enough and apply generically to any and all organizations no matter what they develop, sell, and deliver. However, services marketers faces some additional challenges that further confound the problem:

1. As discussed earlier in the Introduction, services are a dramatically different type of offering than products, and applying traditional marketing approaches to services just doesn't work.

2. In organizations that offer both products and services, services marketing must co-exist with product marketing. Often the two compete internally (and externally) for resources as well as for the mind share of stakeholders. Since the two kinds of marketing have different objectives and different focuses, misalignment, mixed messages, and wasted resources are the result.

3. Often nobody or the wrong people are in charge of services marketing. This is clearly pointed out by Figure 21.

Although the information in that figure is specific to professional services organizations, the results are quite telling. Less than half of respondents in the research had dedicated services marketing personnel (Alexander, 2000). This is a recipe for disaster.

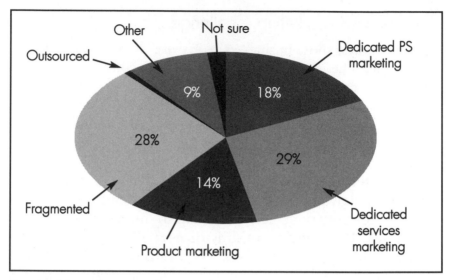

Figure 21: Who is in charge of services marketing?
Source: Alexander, 2000.

Services Marketing Principles

Marketing Maxims

Principles help to create a philosophical framework in which to operate. The following (summarized in Figure 22) are

Figure 22: Services marketing principles.

1. Value is what the customer says it is.
2. Staff is for support.
3. A fast "no" is better than a slow "yes."
4. You can only do a few things well.
5. If you think you know what the customer really wants, you are probably wrong.
6. Everyone's a stakeholder.
7. Innovation is not an accident.
8. Fire and retire.
9. What gets measured…

some proven maxims aimed at helping guide the leaders of services marketing.

VALUE IS WHAT THE CUSTOMER SAYS IT IS

No matter how elegantly designed the service offering, how massive the research effort that defined it, or how expensive its development, the customer doesn't care. The customer only cares about what the benefits are to him or her. The customer defines value.

A useful exercise in helping an organization to discover where it currently adds the most value is to identify its most profitable customers (Whitely and Hessan, 1996). Profit is a strong indicator of value. Analyzing what these select customers find unique and most beneficial in an offering helps those in charge of marketing to understand differentiation possibilities that can be applied elsewhere.

STAFF IS FOR SUPPORT

Marketing staff professionals may be responsible for developing and leading the implementation of many marketing activities, but marketing must be owned by the line to be effective (Ames and Hlavacek, 1989). Berry and Parasuraman (1991) summed it up nicely: "In service businesses the least effective marketing department executives strive to be clever marketers; the most effective executives strive to turn everyone else in the organization into clever marketers" (p. 78).

Everyone whose work touches the customer has marketing responsibility. They should have goals and measures that put accountability to their responsibility. If people's tasks aren't contributing to getting or keeping customers (i.e., to adding value), they are contributing waste (Alexander and Lyons, 1995).

A FAST "NO" IS BETTER THAN A SLOW "YES"

We don't have the luxury to do things 100%, because windows of opportunity are only open so long. All cycle times must be reduced. Decision points must be created and failures quickly dropped. We must make our mistakes faster. Speed is a tool to be used to create competitive advantage (Stalk and Hout, 1990).

In services marketing, speed is most dramatically applied in the rapid prototyping of new offerings. Rapid prototyping means more iteration, more tests, and more milestones to evaluate and make decisions. Rapid prototyping directly impacts long-term product/services profitability (Peters, 1995).

YOU CAN ONLY DO A FEW THINGS REALLY WELL

All organizations have limited resources. We only have so much time and so many opportunities. The concept of core competencies is to do what you do best—develop a few critical capabilities to world-class levels and outsource everything else (Prahalad and Hamel 1990; Quinn, 1992).

The focus on core competencies is bringing about significant changes in business attitudes. Where once the world was black and white—you were either a supplier or a customer to a business—now everything is shades of gray, and the boundaries are blurred. The connectivity between supplier-customer-competitor-partners is formed from the specific realities of a particular situation. Archrivals may compete in one area, sell-buy in another, and create an alliance in a third, depending on the opportunity presented. It is a function of marketing to create, develop, and manage these relationships. Most organizations should strive to make this "alliance-building capability" a core competency.

IF YOU THINK YOU KNOW WHAT THE CUSTOMER REALLY WANTS, YOU ARE PROBABLY WRONG

In some industries such as high-tech, customer expectations change within a six- to twelve-month timeframe. Firms are always in the process of losing touch with their customers. So most of the time when executives say they know their customers' issues and needs in-depth, they are starting down the path of serious trouble.

Issues, expectations, wants, and needs of key customers are too complex to be learned about from standard surveys. The solution is to not take things for granted and to gather new information on a regular basis. One proven way to keep in touch with the voice of the customer is to systematically employ a program of customer visits with cross-functional teams (McQuarrie and McIntyre, 1990).

EVERYONE'S A STAKEHOLDER

Customers, suppliers, and employees are all stakeholders of the marketing process. Everyone should be clearly aware of the marketing strategy and understand their roles and responsibilities in achieving marketing objectives.

Marketing to people inside the organization is just as important as marketing to people outside the organization (Berry and Parasuraman, 1991). Just like customers, inside people must see the value of marketing initiatives for themselves personally. In fact, it may be more important in the high-tech world where many service organizations must educate and persuade sometimes-reluctant product management to re-think their business model.

INNOVATION IS NOT AN ACCIDENT

For organizations that strive to create competitive advantage in the marketplace, innovation can and must be planned for. Innovation is not the "luck meeting opportunity" of a few creative people in the organization. It is not based upon personality traits. It is the rigorous application of a methodology that plans, monitors, and rewards performance that accomplishes innovation goals. Innovation is a function of the company's management system (Robert, 1995).

It is also interesting to ponder that in some fields as much as 80% of innovation comes from customers (Donath, 1992). This demonstrates the criticality of working closely with the lead-users in your market segment whether they are your customers or not (Drucker, 1995). You not only need to know what your customers are thinking and doing, but also what your non-customers are thinking and doing.

FIRE AND RETIRE

If you are green you are growing, if you are ripe you rot. In other words, if you are not moving ahead, you are going backward—you never stay in the same place. As your services organization is constantly learning new and better ways to meet the ever-evolving issues, trends, and expectations of the marketplace, you need to retire some old things then start doing something new. A good rule of thumb is to fire the bottom 20% of your customers and retire 20% of your services offering each year. Make it mandatory that no new services offerings are launched without eliminating an existing one.

WHAT GETS MEASURED...

This is the marketing principle that turns the other principles into a reality—what gets measured gets done. If people have clear personal expectations of what is required by following marketing principles and know that consequences are attached to the results, the probability of their being followed goes up immensely.

For example, some organizations are changing their measuring systems from a focus on customer satisfaction to a focus on customer retention. The results are positive. It has been demonstrated that a 5% increase in customer retention yields an average 50% improvement in profitability (Reichheld and Sasser, 1990). Results like these capture everyone's attention and can focus an entire organization on those relationship and loyalty-building behaviors that yield the greatest returns. Expectations, feedback, and rewards must directly align with the marketing mission of getting and keeping customers.

Importance of Principles

These principles form a framework in which effective services marketing can operate. Value must be defined for both key customers and the organization. Everyone must be responsible and accountable for marketing. Cycle times must be understood and shortened. Core competencies must be operationalized and non-critical functions outsourced. Research "systems" must be put in place to truly understand the most important customers within specific niches. Stakeholders must be identified and actions laid out to inform and influence them. Innovation goals and definitions must be established, tracked, and rewarded.

Now, with the challenges and obstacles duly noted and a set of principles to guide us, let's start our discussion of the key success factors of services marketing, starting with the market message.

Market Message

A market message is the key communication for demonstrating your potential value to your defined market space. It is communicated by everything your organization says and does and helps to shape how customers think about your organization. The result of your market message coupled with customer experience is your brand—both the type of services provider you are seen as and the quality rating that goes along with it. Hence, an appropriate market message is a key component of any marketing system.

What makes a good market message? First, it must align with your services organization's value proposition. Second, it must be "loud" enough so that it is clearly understood by all stakeholders (this is a best practice), both outside and inside the organization. Third, there must be only one message. Customers truly believe that an organization can really be good at only one thing. Claiming you're good at one thing here and another thing there negatively impacts credibility (more on this a little later). Fourth, it must be consistent. The marketing message should change only when the value proposition changes—and this is not something a high-performing services organization does often or without considerable changes in the environment. In most cases, we are talking several years. Customers and employees are easily confused if your "tag line" changes with each new advertising campaign or marketer.

Tag lines are an intricate part of market messages. These short, to-the-point statements speak quite a bit about your capability and vision in only a few words. Ideally they inspire and educate customers by succinctly portraying your strengths and differentiators. In this regard, your tag line should be considered the first chapter of the story you wish to tell future customers. Like a trailer in a movie, your goal is to position the tag line as an emotional hook to lure in new customers by its impact. Ultimately, it's what's behind the tag line being portrayed that really matters (Alexander and Hordes, 2002). The list below shows some examples of services tag lines. You be the judge as to how effectively they motivate, educate, communicate a promise or position, or position a competency that will be remembered.

"As Individual as You"........................Triple-I Systems
                                            Consultants
"Next Things First" ....United Technologies
"We Earn Your Trust Every Day"....Association of CPAs
"The Possibilities are Infinite" ....Fujitsu Consulting
                                            Services
"We're Engineers. We Know
 This Stuff"......................................Phillips 66
"Innovation Delivered"......................Accenture
"World Class IT Solutions"..............MicroAge
"Solutions for Higher Education"....Datatel
"Business and Systems Aligned.
Business Empowered"......................Bearing Point
"The Advantage of Focus"...............Howrey LLP,
                                            Attorneys at Law
"Ideas for a Small Planet" ....IBM

Ponder Point: A recent informal survey conducted by the authors of fifty companies that offer services either as free-standing services organizations or as product-centered companies with support services revealed that only 5% of those interviewed had placed their tag lines on their business cards.

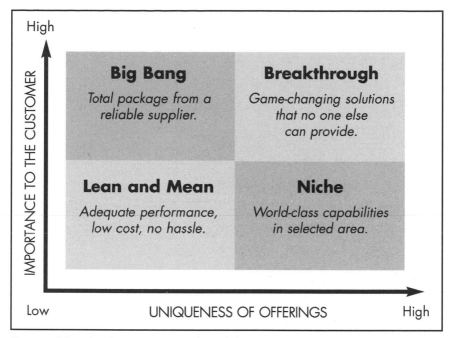

Figure 23: The four strategies and four value propositions.

What a wasted opportunity for something to do that is so simple and quite powerful from a pure marketing perspective.

With that background, let's delve a little deeper into the makeup of a good market message, starting with value propositions.

As a quick review, Figure 23 shows the four value propositions introduced in Chapter 3. Remember that each value proposition is created from what the customer wants and is willing to pay for. Shown are the core elements of the market message associated with each value proposition.

Next, in Figure 24 we've taken the value propositions and added the appropriate market messages:

1. *Just as good but cheaper.* The Lean and Mean strategy calls for a value proposition of adequate performance, low cost, and no hassle. Therefore, those very same factors should be communicated to all stakeholders (both inside and outside the organization).

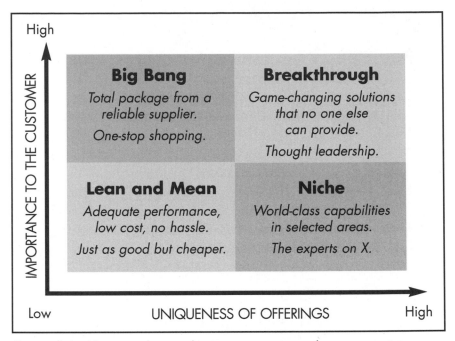

Figure 24: Aligning the marketing message to the appropriate value proposition.

The market message is simple, direct, and to the point: "We may not be fancy, but we are easy to work with and get the job done at a low price." Your people (no Armani suits) and your facilities (used furniture) all reinforce this message.

2. *The experts on X.* The Niche strategy calls for a value proposition of world-class capabilities in selected areas. Thus the appropriate message to the market echoes it back: "We are the experts at *X*. Nobody knows *X* better than we do, nobody." The research papers you present at industry conferences, the white papers available on your Web site, all tout and demonstrate the depth of your specialized knowledge. Depending on your situation, your message may want to communicate that you have been down this road many times before and know all the pitfalls that should be avoided in order to save time and money.

3. *One-stop shopping.* The Big Bang strategy calls for a Total

Solutions value proposition from a reliable supplier. Hence, the mantra appropriate to communicate this is something like this: "Don't worry, we'll take care of everything. You can trust us to do it right. We have a broad breadth of offerings. Lots of experience in big projects. We can manage other suppliers for you."

4. *Thought leadership.* The Breakthrough strategy's value proposition revolves around game-changing ideas from the best and brightest. Therefore, the market message should be something like: "Our innovations will bring you breakthroughs in performance." This is reinforced by an almost elitist attitude that permeates the company's culture. Members of such organizations are expected to publish articles, white papers, and books, as well as speak at high-level business conferences on leading-edge concepts and models. You are getting across the idea that only the best are a part of your organization. Only A players from the top schools help shape decisions. There is no second team in this organization.

Brand Building

Branding is all about getting your market message heard and believed. It includes educating your marketplace on your core services offerings and packaging these attributes for maximum market effectiveness. No matter what strategy you are pursuing, word-of-mouth and word-of-mouse are the ideal promoters, as nothing is stronger than having customers tout your value, particularly respected high-level executives from respected high-impact organizations.

As a services organization, your people are the first and foremost representatives of your services brand. Everyone on your staff communicates your brand in many ways. The way staff members talk about what the organization stands for, the way they listen to customers' concerns, and the way they respond to those concerns make a powerful impression. Also, ensuring a consistent look and feel in brochures, Web pages, stationery,

Table IV: Brand Building: Outside

Tactic	Vendor	TS Provider	Specialist	Game Changer
Great networks	5	5	5	5
Get good PR	2	4	3	5
Publish books	–5	4	4	5
Publish research	–5	0	5	5
Publish white papers	–3	3	5	5
Publish newsletter	0	3	3	4
Publish articles	0	3	5	3
Give speeches	0	5	5	5
Executive briefings	–5	3	0	5
Sponsor causes	3	3	3	3
Do seminars	0	3	5	3
Sponsor events	2	5	3	0
Do lunch & learns	–5	2	3	0
Direct mail	4	0	3	–1
Trade show booths	5	2	3	–2
Advertise	5	2	3	–3

Legend: 5=must do   0=neutral   –5=must avoid

and project communications creates a sense that the organization is grounded and well organized. Consistently doing good work (meeting expectations) and occasionally doing awesome work (greatly exceeding expectations in targeted situations) are cornerstones of brand building.

The types of promotion you use to communicate your brand are again dependent upon your services strategy and the services offerings you want to emphasize.

There are many different activities that a services organization can undertake to consciously build its brand. All take time and all take resources. Table IV looks at a number of possible brand-building activities and scores their potential worth according to the services strategy being pursued. Note that all types of services providers gain from networking—establishing personal connections with a number of influential people. Also note that while a brand-building tactic for one type of strategy could be quite helpful, that same tactic for a services organization pursing a different strategy might actually harm brand-building efforts. Of course, multiple tactics should be happening concurrently.

Game Changers need to communicate their leading-edge concepts. After building a network of high-level contacts, the most prestigious way to do that is through research studies, white papers, and speaking engagements. PR is another important element of the communication arsenal, and individuals from game-changing organizations should be regularly quoted in business media and noted as experts in their particular fields. A quality newsletter (free or by paid subscription) is another strong credibility builder as long as its content is built upon innovative concepts. An attractive Web site helps, and is made especially impressive if it offers a vast library of publications to download. Advertising and booths are too pedestrian for these players and should be avoided. Thought leaders speak at conferences; they don't sponsor them.

For the most part, Specialists should try to emulate the brand-building approach outlined for Game Changers, as their main thrust is to demonstrate special expertise. However, because Specialists deal with a more hands-on type of customer, both booths at trade shows and targeted advertising in industry journals make a lot of sense to pursue.

Total Solutions Providers never want to lose the opportunity to compete for a big deal. Hence, it is not only important that they continually build relationships as high and as wide in target accounts as possible, but they must get their names out continually so as not to be left out by accounts they haven't penetrated yet. Therefore, a good strategy for these players is to sponsor high-visibility events where lots of the right prospects will be bombarded with their communications. Advertising is an appropriate element of their communication mix and should focus on case studies that not only tout results but also demonstrate reliability.

For the most part, Vendors fare best by using the time-proven approaches of product marketing promotion: advertising, direct mail, trade shows, etc. Speaking and publishing certainly won't hurt, but probably aren't worth the investment.

Brand building doesn't stop with market-facing efforts—smart services marketers spend as much time inside as outside. The four steps listed in Figure 25 guide this approach.

Unless a brand-building activity is in your plan, it probably won't get done. Build a separate section just on internal brand building into your services marketing plan, complete with goals, key activities, budgets, timeframes, and so on. Monitor and adjust as needed.

Just as your external brand building is bent on selling current and potential customers on the value of your offerings and your organization, your internal brand building should be focused on persuading stakeholders within your organization. Everyone must know (and believe in) your market message and be able to succinctly communicate the benefits of your organization any time, any place. This is always important but absolutely vital when your organization is transitioning from a product-centered organization to an s-business (more on this in Chapter 10). In this situation you will be facing many skeptical people who will have to change their image of services if the organizational change is to take place successfully.

All internal communications about marketing should focus on three things—what you are doing, why you are doing it, and the benefit to stakeholders (the customer, your company, and the individual employee). Furthermore, the case needs to be

Figure 25: Brand building: inside.

1. Build an internal branding plan.
2. Regularly sell the benefits.
3. Involve all employees.
4. Recognize and reward contributions.

built that marketing is everyone's responsibility. To accomplish this objective, this message must be repeated over and over, just like with outside stakeholders. A good way to do this is to share the results of external marketing efforts on a quarterly basis (via intranet, internal newsletters, breakfast-luncheons, brief presentations on various department meetings).

Another good approach to branding internally is to solicit input from all employees. First, you'll glean some good, usable information on the cheap; second, the mere act of involvement helps to form commitment. Ask for employees' ideas on improving brand building both outside and inside the organization, and communicate back the results. Suggest ideas about how all employees can help promote the organization, and provide the tools for them to do so.

Finally, recognize and reward worthwhile employee contributions. This helps increase support further and demonstrates that marketing is an important element of the business.

Credibility

Just as corporate culture is the result of strategy and how it is implemented, credibility is the end product of the impact of your market message, the success of your brand-building efforts, and how your organization and your services have been experienced. The market message can be fine-tuned, while the services organization's credibility can only be measured and tracked.

When customers grant you credibility (believe in your brand), they are more willing to trust your firm in the development of a mutual value exchange. Some services brands carry enormous market weight. IBM Global Services, GE, McKinsey, Accenture, and several software companies have leveraged their professional services market plays into 40% margins. (However, see the sidebar "The Blessing (or Curse) of a Strong Product Brand" for some difficulties faced by product-centered companies in establishing a services brand.)

The Blessing (or Curse) of a Strong Product Brand

For services organization that are a part of a product-centered organization with a strong brand (e.g., Xerox, Kodak, Dell), an interesting dilemma occurs. On the one hand, assuming the product brand is perceived as positive, it lends instant awareness and credibility to the services organization. In most situations (and without the need for proof), the services organization will be seen as possessing strong capabilities related to product support services, and possibly given the title of best in class without further thought. This can be an enormous advantage and plays perfectly to the services organization pursuing a Niche strategy. The key in this situation is to make every effort to leverage that strength and to co-brand—to build a services brand that links closely to the product side of the company.

The disadvantage in this is if your strategy calls for you to wander from your product, expanding services in areas not directly associated (by customers) with your core product business. For example, consider a product support services organization that wants to get heavily involved in professional services. Often the customer will have a negative reaction: "You guys are experts at *X*. What can you possibly know about *Y*? You should stick to your knitting." This scenario calls for the delicate act of having your cake and eating it too by careful co-branding.

Just as co-branding with a strong product big brother is a powerful tool, lesser-known services organizations can often gain credibility by association with other (non-competitor) companies with broad awareness and universal acceptance as a market leader. Sponsoring events that include world-class organizations is the classic model for using this approach. For example, say you are a Niche player in the network security field with limited market-place visibility. Sponsoring a symposium on security and having executives from organizations such as Cisco and Microsoft, a U.S. Defense Department spokesperson, and an MIT professor on the speaking platform will immediately help build your brand by association. Better yet if you are already a partner with the big-name presenters. Better still if they will mention your expertise in a case example or two during their presentations.

Credibility helps to compress selling cycle times, as a positive reputation opens doors and lowers resistance to buying. Hence, credibility (via the brand) is a decision-making short cut. This is extremely important, as often the buyers of sophisticated services or complex solutions don't have the technical knowledge to compare different offerings. The must make decisions based upon the indicators of future success, and a positive reputation is one of the most critical of those indicators. The results are important: There is a direct relationship between a strong brand and higher profit margins and also a direct relationship between an organization's marketplace credibility and the ability to hire top talent.

Figure 26 shows the ten factors of a credibility assessment that can provide you with almost instantaneous feedback on the quality of your services marketing efforts today and their probable success in the future (Alexander and Hordes, 2002)

The first four factors directly reflect your credibility performance to date. Each step is progressive, going from awareness, to understanding, to competitive position. Of course, scoring a 5 on Question 4 is where you'd like to be—being recognized as the leader in implementing your selected services strategy.

The next six factors indicate the strength of your credibility in the future. Looking at which of these factors are in place

	Strongly disagree	Strongly agree
1. Most prospective clients in your defined market have heard of you.	1 2 3 4 5 6 7 8 9 10	
2. Most prospective clients in your defined market have a clear perception about you (what you do and how well you do it).	1 2 3 4 5 6 7 8 9 10	
3. Most prospective clients have a favorable perception toward your PSO.	1 2 3 4 5 6 7 8 9 10	
4. You have the reputation as the leader in your field.	1 2 3 4 5 6 7 8 9 10	
5. Your executives recognize that the brand is a vital asset.	1 2 3 4 5 6 7 8 9 10	
6. All "packaging" (people, communications, pricing, materials, offices, etc.) convey the same message.	1 2 3 4 5 6 7 8 9 10	
7. Your PSO makes a conscious effort to delight customers on select projects.	1 2 3 4 5 6 7 8 9 10	
8. Branding campaigns (inside and out) are aggressively funded.	1 2 3 4 5 6 7 8 9 10	
9. Brand awareness is tracked.	1 2 3 4 5 6 7 8 9 10	
10. Brand quality is tracked.	1 2 3 4 5 6 7 8 9 10	

TOTAL SCORE = _____

Figure 26: Credibility audit.

today will give you a pretty fair indication of where your credibility will be tomorrow. Take a couple minutes and complete the assessment for your organization. How do you shape up?

Pricing

Price must match strategy (Figure 27). As we've discussed, in order to play the game, Vendors must be low price (or ideally) the lowest price. Pricing pressure will always be a part of the negotiating game that occurs when two or more Total Solutions Providers slug it out for huge contracts. In these cases, prices

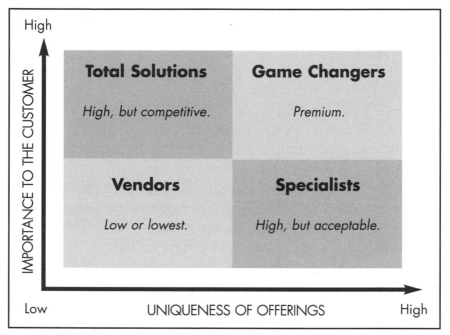

Figure 27: Services pricing.

can be higher than competitors, but must be seen as competitive. Specialists are begrudged higher prices that customers don't mind paying unless the customers feel they are being gouged. In those situations, they will pay your price for now (what choice do they have?) but will aggressively investigate other options and gleefully drop you once an alternative is found. Customers expect to pay a premium for game-changing services. In fact, customers will puzzle over prices not seen as "high enough" and question the value potential being offered. Game Changers want customers to tell their peers: "Are they expensive? You bet! But worth every penny."

Of course pricing has a big impact on your financial performance. Here are a few ideas to get your pricing right:

1. Align your pricing philosophy with your services strategy. As noted above, different strategies demand different attitudes toward pricing and price is not a prime buying factor except for Vendors.

2. Stay up-to-date on industry pricing, especially in regard to competitors pursuing the same strategy as you. Conduct formal market pricing intelligence every six months. You want your pricing to be at the "high end" but within an acceptable range of your best competitors.

3. If you charge by time and materials (we don't recommend this), segment price by the talent levels of your professional staff (higher capability, higher rate) and charge extra when "above and beyond" efforts are required.

4. Except for Vendors, always make your first choice value-based pricing in which you are stating one price for the accomplishment of high-impact, mutually agreed upon customer benefits no matter what effort is required.

5. Along with a value-based price, consider providing an option in which you assume some risk and link compensation to the accomplishment of objectives (include an upside for surpassing goals). This demonstrates confidence, separates you from the competition, and reinvents the buying-purchasing paradigm.

Services Portfolio Management

So far in our discussion we've outlined that the services marketing staff must face the challenging tasks of fitting the organization's services offerings into the most appropriate strategy quadrant. This is a very important task, but one that must be continually adjusted to the constant movement in the marketplace. To effectively manage the services portfolio, services marketers must accept the concepts of erosion, abandonment, and replacement. They must also understand how to classify the services being offered in terms of customer familiarity.

Erosion

The sad truth is that as familiarity with a services offering increases, its uniqueness dwindles as more competitors enter the fray, slowly but relentlessly pushing your service from right to

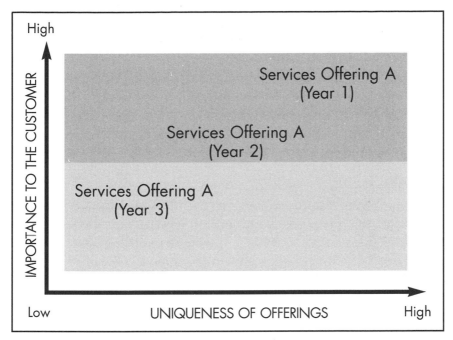

Figure 28: The relentless erosion. Example.

left on the uniqueness scale, commoditizing a once unique offering, and lowering its profit potential. At the same time there is always movement on the importance axis, usually a slow top to bottom movement as today's hot topics (e.g., reengineering, Y2K) become tomorrow's old hat. However, a change in events can elevate the importance of services that have been around a while (e.g., security, remote monitoring).

Shown in Figure 28 is a representative example. Services Offering A when just introduced was seen as an innovative approach to dealing with a mission-critical issue in the market space served by this services provider. However, competitors quickly reacted to this new opportunity with services offerings of their own—ones remarkably similar to Services Offering A. Furthermore, changes in the marketplace slowly started to reduce the importance of the problems and opportunities that Services Offering A was designed to address. So in only a couple of years, Services Offering A went from being a one-of-a-kind, high-impact (and, hopefully, a very high-profit) offering to a commodity of medium importance being fiercely competed against by a host of competitors.

This is exactly what makers of high-tech products have been facing for years, although their "time to erosion" has been measured in months (sometimes weeks) and not years. This doesn't seem fair, but that's the way it is and services businesses are no different. What are the ramifications?

Abandonment

For *all* organizations to be successful, they must follow an approach of "planned abandonment" (Drucker, 1995), which means that on a regular basis and using established criteria, they must drop certain services offerings (or possibly entire services portfolios) while adding fresh offerings in their stead. Psychologically this is difficult to do, as most people hate to give up anything, preferring to just add more to the plate. But in terms of running a business this is even more difficult as the usual ideal time for abandonment is right about the time the services offering is the most profitable—a time when you've finally figured it out and you are at the top of your game!

For Vendors, planned abandonment is the least painful. Players in the other three quadrants are continually introducing new services and over time they all turn into commodities. Hence, there are opportunities coming up all the time in which the Vendors' advantages in efficiencies give them big advantages. They can let the numbers drive abandonment—using sales volume and gross profit margin to cut out the lowest-performing offerings as new, potentially higher-performing commodity offerings take their place.

For Specialists, abandonment usually comes slowly as there are fewer competitors and the lower importance of the issues they deal with keeps them off the radarscope of the 800-pound gorillas of the industry. However, no matter the timeframe, uniqueness eventually goes away and the Specialists must bring out new services on a regular basis while eliminating older ones.

For Total Solutions Providers, planned abandonment is a big problem, as a lot of resources have been poured into creating the capabilities to deliver on big-time projects. Think for example of all the cost and turmoil required to "time the market"—to deliver on Y2K, then gear up for ERP, then e-business, then CRM, and so on and so on. It is painful to abandon once highly successful services offerings, then have to cope with the need for retraining, but it is even more painful to not catch the next big business wave.

For Game Changers, it is also very difficult to let go of services offerings that only yesterday may have been heralded as the great concepts in management. Pride of ownership steps in. Yet hanging on to yesterday's ideas deals a sharp blow to organizations touting innovation. Game Changers must continually change their own "games" as well.

Replacement

Erosion and abandonment mean that every organization expecting to be a player tomorrow must have strong capabilities in creating and launching new services today. However, as pointed out earlier in this chapter, most organizations aren't very effective at it. A big part of the reason for that is they use the wrong approach for the wrong type of services offering.

Customer Familiarity

Classifying services based upon customer familiarity is particularly helpful when introducing new services offerings as it has a big impact on what works and what doesn't (Alexander, 1996). Familiarity is a helpful distinction since customers make judgments and decisions based upon both the perceived value of using a services offering and the confidence felt that this value will materialize. Customer familiarity affects both. The three categories of customer familiarity are existing, emerging, and breakthrough services.

Existing services are ones that customers are very familiar with. Based upon personal experience, customers probably have a good understanding of a service's functionality and certainly know their own likes and dislikes in regard to it, along with their ideas for its improvement.

Emerging services are those which customers have no personal experience with, but know about from trade magazines, trade shows, or discussions with other users. Possibly a service has been used for another application and is being considered for something applicable to the customers' needs. In this situation, customers can project (with some degree of accuracy) their own thoughts and ideas about the new service. Customers have enough knowledge to think about the potential value of the service to their own unique situations.

Breakthrough services are totally new. In these cases, customers have no experience and no frame of reference for comparison or contrast, or for projecting a new service's utility. For example, a few years ago remote diagnostics* could have been classified as a breakthrough service. It changed the game at that time, as in many cases it eliminated the need for service visits when problems arose and, better yet, it was able to predict problems before they occurred. Thus the potential was there to increase system uptime, improve customer satisfaction, and lower cost all at once. Beware the services provider caught off guard by this new service! However, competitors of all types quickly followed suit and remote diagnostics went from being a breakthrough service to an emerging service. As customers of all types became more familiar with remote diagnostics through personal experience, or talking to peers, or reading articles, the service became highly familiar to all those in the services industry and is now a standard existing service.

As you'd expect, Vendors are only interested in existing services offerings. The primary focus of Total Solutions Providers is emerging services. Both Specialist and Game Changers are most interested in breakthrough services. See Figure 29.

---

* It is interesting to note that as this book was being written, remote diagnostics were being reinvented (and hence moving out of the Vendor quadrant) as new technologies such as DRM (*device relationship management*) were being introduced.

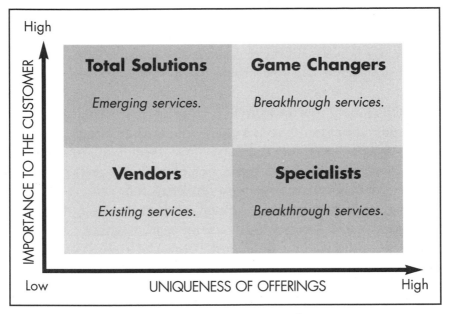

Figure 29: Launching new services: primary focus.

Launching New Services

Here you are dealing with the impact of customer familiarity on the services being introduced (see Table V).

Approach

When launching new services where existing services already exist, the marketing approach is to replace the existing offering

Table V: The Impact of Customer Familiarity on
New Services Introductions

	Existing	Emerging	Breakthrough
Approach	Live with the rules	Change the rules	Change the game
Research Methods	Quantitative emphasis	Qualitative emphasis	Observe and speculate
Preparation	Rigorous planning	Plan but experiment	Ready, fire, aim

by providing a combination of benefits that are easier, better, faster, or cheaper than the existing offering. Basic expectations are already in place. In this scenario, you live within the rules of the existing game but operate more efficiently. This is Vendor country.

When launching a new services offering that is emerging, the marketing approach is to get there first and convince the customer/prospect to trust your capabilities to deliver. You change the rules of the game by creating new standards of expectations. This is the country of Total Solution Providers.

When you are launching a breakthrough services, the marketing approach is to drastically alter a customer process or way of doing business. You don't just break the rules; you totally change the game by introducing significant innovation. This is Game Changers' country.

Research Methods

Categorizing services based on customer familiarity has special significance for the conductors of market research. If we believe that customers' perceptions are their reality and that people will (most of the time) act rationally, the more familiar customers are with a services offering, the more accurate the information gathered from them (assuming the right research methods are deployed). The less familiar customers are with a potential service, the less credence must be given to their comments about the need for it or its potential value or success. When put on the spot with a question that they don't know the answer to, most people will not say they don't know. They will speculate to save face or fabricate a response for the sake of being polite or trying to be helpful. Often they will try to guess what the researcher really wants and try to respond with information that supports their assumption.

So with existing services, traditional quantitative marketing research methods are preferred. They are both adequate and the most cost-effective. With emerging products, quantitative techniques can add value, but only to augment qualitative research.

The thick, rich information gathered through personal interviews and focus groups must be the primary research methods. With very unfamiliar services, usage must be inferred. The best way to do this is through actual observation of customers in scenarios where the service offering has potential application (Martin, 1995). By watching how people actually behave and the problems they encounter and solve, qualified researchers can understand the likelihood of the success of very new services. Also, it is important to remember that predicting the application of breakthrough services cannot be truly scientific. Hardly any truly revolutionary products ended up being utilized the way their inventors intended (Drucker, 1996). Researchers must speculate, infer, and make their best guesses.

Preparation

Introducing existing services calls for rigorous planning and meticulous follow-through. The proof is in following procedures step-by-step. Emerging services call for creating and following a process that encourages multiple iterations and experimentation (Alexander, 1995). Flexibility is vital. With breakthrough services, a detailed plan just gets in the way. "Ready-fire-aim" conveys the spirit of introducing potential breakthrough products—just do it. The key is to quickly get prototypes into the hands of lead customers and let them test and experiment.

Best Practices

Here are the twelve marketing core practices (summarized in Figure 30) from the s-business study (Alexander, 2002):

1. *A services marketing plan is in place.* This is an absolute must for any s-business.
2. *The services value proposition is understood clearly by all stakeholders.* Make the market message and the services brand building drive home your value proposition both outside and inside the organization

A services marketing plan is in place.**

The services value proposition is clearly understood by all stakeholders.**

"Value-based" pricing is the most common pricing method.**

A dedicated services marketing staff is in place.*

Ongoing market research is conducted.*

Information on services is just one click away from the home page.*

Customers are segmented by loyalty and profitability.*

Building the brand and communicating key market messages are organizational objectives.

Branding campaigns are funded aggressively.

All "packaging" (people, communications, pricing, physical environment) conveys the same message.

The services brand is congruent with the product brand.

The external and internal market messages are the same.

Figure 30: Marketing best practices.

* Statistically proven s-business differentiator from product-centered company.
** Statistically proved practice of top-performing s-businesses.

3. *"Value-based" pricing is the most common pricing method.* Buyers buy benefits. Link your services and solutions to the expected business impact of their delivery.

4. *A dedicated services marketing staff is in place.* Services are different than products. Don't allow product marketing to market services.

5. *Ongoing market research is conducted.* Environmental scanning, competitive analysis, voice of the customer research, and brand quality research should be conducted at least twice a year. We recommend involving services organization personnel plus using outside expertise.

6. *Information on services is only one click away from the home page.* For s-businesses that sell products, make sure that any visitor to your Web site can access services information in just

one click. Make it easy to learn (and buy) services in any way the customer wishes.

7. *Customers are segmented by loyalty and profitability.* Is there anything better than *loyal and profitable customers!*

8. *Building the brand and communicating key market messages are organizational objectives.* This should always be a top priority. Brand is everything!

9. *Branding campaigns are funded aggressively.* Be cheap at your own peril! If you need to spend money spend it here.

10. *All "packaging" (people, communications, pricing, physical environment) conveys the same message.* Not following this practice creates confusion. Audit to make sure that there is alignment.

11. *The services brand is congruent with the product brand.* Hey, can't we all just get along!

12. *The external and internal market messages are the same.* One message, one voice, all audiences.

Conclusion

Bottom line, it is the role of s-business marketing to make the strategy come alive. Defining the right market message, relentlessly building the brand, getting pricing right, and managing the services portfolio all are critical enablers. A set of principles and some established best practices help to guide the process.

Chapter 5

Selling S-Business: The Ten Commandments

RESEARCH FACTOID: Only 13% of services executives are fully satisfied that their services salespeople are selling the right offerings to the right customers in the right way.

PONDER POINT: *Everyone* is responsible for selling services.

PURPOSE: Chapter 5 will help you to:

- Leverage the business development process to get more and better business faster
- Learn the ten commandments of selling professional services
- Understand best services selling practices
- Align the selling approach to the services strategy

Starting in Chapter 3 we've demonstrated that, rightly or wrongly, customers classify services providers into different categories and have different expectations of them, since each has different buying patterns. Therefore, we need a strategy and a

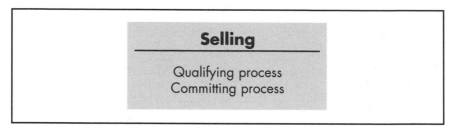

Figure 31: The selling lever.

marketing approach that aligns with those different customer perceptions. This chapter builds on that point as we realize that to be successful we must sell the way that customers want to buy and this has big implications for capability requirements and selling implementation.

In this chapter we'll discuss the s-business selling lever with its two component processes of qualifying and commitment (Figure 31). We'll talk about the selling services performance gap and then introduce the enablers of selling services—the business development process that is important in selling any type of services offering. Then we'll share a set of rules, ten "commandments" that apply to anyone selling sophisticated, important services. Finally, we'll take into consideration the implications of the type of services strategy on the selling approach—selling how buyers want to buy.

Figure 32 outlines the business development process and its prime objective of getting, growing, and keeping clients. So far in this book we have been using the terms *prospect, customer,* and *client* rather loosely. When it comes to selling, it pays to be more precise. Here are some definitions:

- Leads: all the potential buyers in your selected market place
- Suspects: leads that have expressed an interest in your offerings
- Prospects: suspects that meet your qualification standards
- Customers: prospects that have purchased your offerings
- Clients: customers that exhibit loyalty to you, your offerings, and your organization

The promoting process, turning leads into suspects, is mar-

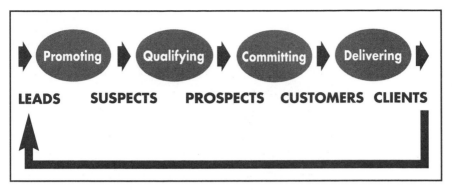

Figure 32: The business development process: getting, growing, and keeping clients.

keting's responsibility. Your brand-building and communication activities should create awareness and generate interest so that suspects contact you. Although vital to business development, marketing services was covered in detail in Chapter 4 and only limited comments will be given in this chapter.

Qualifying (Figure 31), turning suspects into prospects, compares potential customers to your ideal business criteria. Committing (Figure 31) takes prospects and turns them into customers—organizations that have purchased from you one time. The delivery process takes customers and (if done effectively) turns them into clients, or organizations that buy from you again and again and again. Note that delivery is often not associated with business development as the selling has been done up front and the realm of delivery is meeting expectations on time, up to quality, and within budget. This is all true, but the delivery process done well is the best time to get easy, new, profitable sales. Everything in this chapter relates to how to conduct these three processes easier, better, and faster yielding more clients and a more profitable s-business.

The Sales Performance Gap

Research shows that only 13% of professional services managers are fully satisfied that their professional services salespeople are

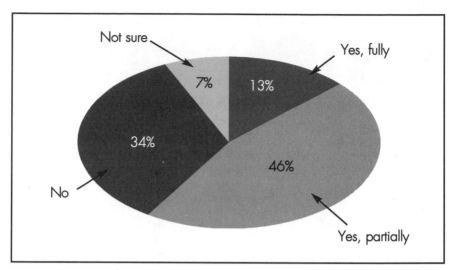

Figure 33: Satisfaction with salespeople's performance.
Source: Alexander, 2000.

selling the right offerings to the right clients in the right way
(Figure 33) (Alexander, 2000). Field reality supports this finding,
as the "low-hanging fruit" most often uncovered from services
organization performance audits are opportunities in sales effectiveness. It is here that smart investments can yield both rapid
and often dramatic improvements in performance.

The Ten Commandments

*Note: Although the following discussion of the ten commandments of
selling services is written from the perspective of professional services
offerings important to the buying organization and sometimes includes
a bundle of offerings (Total Solutions), it will have value to all services
organizations no matter what strategy they are trying to implement.
However, due to the nature of the Lean and Mean strategy,
Commandments 1, 3, 4, and 5, are not relevant to Vendors.*

Ten directives, or "commandments," provide the framework
from which to first understand sales performance problems and
opportunities and then implement positive changes. The
process is simple, the problems understood, and most of the

Commandments	Strongly disagree			Strongly agree		Don't know
1. Clarify complex customer issues.	1	2	3	4	5	☐
2. Communicate the invisible.	1	2	3	4	5	☐
3. Customize each solution.	1	2	3	4	5	☐
4. Commit high-level executives to action.	1	2	3	4	5	☐
5. Coordinate the selling team.	1	2	3	4	5	☐
6. Compress the cycle time of selling.	1	2	3	4	5	☐
7. Concentrate on the stars.	1	2	3	4	5	☐
8. Control the cost of sales.	1	2	3	4	5	☐
9. Commercialize the sales promise.	1	2	3	4	5	☐
10. Continually learn and grow.	1	2	3	4	5	☐

Figure 34: The ten commandments of selling professional services —survey.

Source: Alexander and Hordes, 2002a.

remedies straightforward. There is one caveat, however: Just like the Ten Commandments used in the biblical sense, there are no exceptions—to excel in professional services selling, you must do all ten well.

Figure 34 lists the ten commandments in a survey format. Take the quick diagnostic to gain a macro-understanding of your current state of professional services sales effectiveness. First, determine your services organization's ability today to live up to each of the ten commandments, then compute your total score and overall average.

Congratulations on all scores of 4 or 5, as these are areas of strength—keep doing what you are doing. For now, don't worry about items you scored 3 on, as your resources need to be targeted toward any commandments where you scored 1 or 2. This is where immediate opportunity lies.

(Note that when respondents to this audit are brutally honest, it is rare for an organization to receive a total score over 35. In addition, it is very common for services organizations to have three or more commandments rated at a sub-par level, so don't be disappointed in your scoring—that's one reason why improving sales effectiveness is an area of low-hanging fruit.)

Here is an explanation of each commandment, including best practices, many of which can be implemented immediately. Remember to target your attention toward those commandments where you scored less than a 3.

The First Commandment: Clarify Complex Customer Issues
Ponder Point: If the issues were easy, the customer wouldn't need you.

The issues of professional services are usually ambiguous, often interrelated, and sometimes baffling. That's why your professional service organization (PSO) is involved—to provide not only subject-matter expertise, but also critical thinking coupled with a neutral perspective gained from multiple engagements dealing with very similar and also very different situations. This is where the sales professional and his or her selling team have the greatest opportunity not only to add value through communicating capabilities and enabling relationships but also to actually create value through intellect and experience combined with just the right level of creativity. This initial phase of account involvement is where the professional services sales professional earns his or her keep.

Clearly identifying and defining the problem is over half the battle. If you don't get this part of the selling process right, your chances of getting the business are slim. Worse, though, is defining the issues incorrectly but still getting the engagement. In this scenario, all you can hope for is discovering your error before it is too late, apologizing profusely, and pouring resources into the fray in an attempt at service recovery. The worst case, however, and one that appears to be happening more and more, is that the wrong solution is implemented, the customer is highly dissatisfied with the outcome, your firm loses money trying to correct the uncorrectable, and you end up with a great loss of time, money, and industry reputation (Kennedy Information Research Group, 1999).

The logical path to clarifying complex customer issues is simple:

- Analyze existing data; review current systems, models, and procedures; and question account personnel to clearly understand the critical business issues.
- Listen intently throughout the process to determine which of those issues your services organization (with or without alliance partners) can effectively address.
- Formulate a framework that succinctly defines critical business issues, the implications for not addressing them, and the positive impact of correct action.

BEST PRACTICES

Here are some actions you can take to make sure you get it right the first time:

- Standardize and routinely utilize a "mini-needs assessment" early on to gather account information thoroughly and systematically. Include a broad base of account stakeholders made up of executives, functional heads, technical experts, and users.
- Create and formalize an account-probing strategy. Make the best use of your time and account personnel by asking planned "high-yield" questions, with appropriate follow-ups to crystallize and deepen understanding.
- Enlist the account in the process. Involving key account personnel in gathering the information not only improves data quality but also builds commitment to your later recommendations.
- Implement team selling (see the Fifth Commandment). It is rare that one person has all the knowledge and experience required, so combine people from sales with those having technical know-how, business acumen, and industry experience in the data-collecting process.
- Capture and convey internal learning and experiences through a user-friendly knowledge management system. Make it easy for everyone who comes into contact with customers to learn from experiences.

- Train everyone involved in selling (and that should be nearly everyone) on listening, questioning, and problem analysis. Provide personal coaching as needed.

The Second Commandment: **Communicate the Invisible**

Ponder Point: The more intangible the offering, the more unease within the buyer.

Experience has proven that the more "invisible" the offering, the more challenging the task of communicating both the problem and the solution side of the equation (Alexander, 1996; Levitt, 1981). Here is where the premise that "a good salesperson can sell anything" meets its demise—for many product salespeople are ineffective at selling services of any type. In fact, our experience shows that even with a thorough realignment of sales objectives and compensation coupled with intensive training and supportive coaching, only about two out of three product salespeople (including the very best) successfully make the transition to selling services. This is a sad but true reality.

Much of the cause for this lack of service offerings sales performance stems from the fundamental differences between products and services discussed in the Introduction. The implications of these distinctions are that different sales skills, knowledge, and mindsets are required to sell each type of offering. Furthermore, an attribute that might be a strength in selling products could well be a weakness in selling a service. Different strokes for different folks, as they say.

BEST PRACTICES:

Here are some proven actions to address this critical challenge:

- Create a dedicated services sales force.
- Tangibilize intangibles by turning feelings into facts and concepts into cash. Use analogies and stories to help accounts grasp your meanings. Use testimonials and financial worksheets to make your concepts, capabilities, and results real.
- Create feature-benefit-results profiles for all services offerings. All solutions need to be tailored to the situation (see the

Third Commandment); however, 80% of what is appropriate in one situation will be relevant in others.

- Develop a proposal-writing template complete with examples of well-written prose. Designate (and reward) proposal writers who have strong communications skills.

- Forget about off-the-shelf, generic training packages or the $99 ballroom extravaganzas. Use high-quality, services-specific sales training systems tailored to your industry and your organization.

When integrating product sales personnel into the services selling equation:

- Adjust the sales management support system to reflect new expectations and shift compensation.

- Heavily incent the desired services sales behavior for at least the first six months.

- When selling "solutions" (both products and services) always utilize team selling. Select an account manager and clearly define team member roles and responsibilities.

- Train and coach, train and coach, train and coach.

- Realize from the outset that some product salespeople will not successfully make the transition to services selling. Provide everyone the opportunity to succeed, but address this issue head-on, and help find those unsuited for services selling positions elsewhere inside or outside your organization.

The Third Commandment: Customize Each Solution

Ponder Point: Each touch point with a new customer presents an opportunity to intensify his or her uniqueness.

On the one hand, the account is looking for a services organization that is *the* expert in its industry, knowledgeable about its specific problems, and well-versed in all the nuances that its type of business entails. On the other hand, the account *knows* its own situation is unique and abhors the thought of having a cookie-cutter solution pulled down from the shelf and used to cut into its dough (pun intended).

Furthermore, the more seasoned the professional services salesperson, the more he or she realizes that the majority of issues and opportunities, problems, and options are similar across businesses, geographies, and industries. When these old pros hear the words, "But our situation is different," their first inclination may be to don a knowing smile and wittily educate the account that they've seen it all before. Don't let them do it! All of us, to some degree, relish our uniqueness, and professional services salespeople initially perceived as outside experts there to help quickly will be seen as a cocky "know-it-alls," there to show off, when they attempt to deny another person's view of reality. The psychologists call this "invalidation," and the normal reaction is quite strong, quite negative, and often quite lasting.

Finally, the problem is compounded by every organization's desire to drive efficiency through "productizing" offerings. As soon as the truly unique project is completed successfully, the search starts to find other accounts in which the solution can be applied. While the idea is a good one, as it embraces the concepts of continuous learning and leveraging capabilities, it must be balanced with the realization that the better job the organization does of ker-chunking the solution, the more quickly it is viewed as being generic. Customers don't pay premium prices for generic offerings. So even if your offering is "me-too" in most respects, it is up to the salesperson to tailor its application in a way that the account perceives as unique just to them.

BEST PRACTICES

- In *all* proposals and letters of engagement, first demonstrate a clear understanding of the account's situation before outlining recommendations or solutions.
- Use account terms, phrases, and examples in all account communications.
- Utilize industry data and trends to show linkage to the client's business.
- Leverage tried-and-true methodologies and processes that have

flexibility and can expand or reduce depending on the scope of the engagement, time allocated, and budget parameters.

• Be aware of balance. Demonstrate related experience, yet respect and point out areas of uniqueness.

The Fourth Commandment: Commit High-Level Executives to Action

Ponder Point: Buyer motivation is based on just two things: confidence and urgency.

By definition (ours, at least), professional services is all about addressing the few, critical business issues of accounts that, if handled correctly, make a significant organizational impact. This, of course, is the domain of top management—those busy, focused, no-nonsense folks responsible for the health of the organization.

For salespeople used to talking technology innovation to department heads or combating purchasing agents over discounts, this is often a rude awakening. The executive faced with this type of dialogue quickly will point the salesperson back to the elevator and suggest that she or he go talk to Terri in the IT department or Fred in purchasing. It's not that executives don't necessarily care, it's that they don't have time for the nitty-gritty. Their job is to plot the course and navigate the ship, not buy the supplies or maintain the vessel.

Furthermore, techniques found successful in dealing at lower levels of the organization just don't cut it when on the helm. For example, starting an initial meeting with a department head with the statement, "Tell me about your critical issues," may yield good results and start positioning you as a sales professional. However, the busy exec has no time or desire to educate the uneducated and will grimace when confronted with this probe. He/she expects sales professionals to assume the role of consultant from the first minute of the first meeting, bringing fresh and useful information relevant to their situation. Only then will he/she consider taking valuable time to share with you the issues.

BEST PRACTICES

- Think, speak, write, and talk in business-ese. Translate and net-out all technical issues into what executives care about—business performance.
- Link your solutions back to the critical business issues of the particular executive you are dealing with. Whether talking about systems integration, market research, or talent acquisition, connect your solution directly to revenue growth, market share, cost reduction, new market entry—whatever your research uncovered as the drivers for a particular executive.
- Use your face cards when required. Sometimes CEOs prefer to talk to other CEOs. Use your managing partners and other executives when you think it will impact the sales process.
- Never meet with an executive without doing your homework and having something of interest to present.
- Master the art of the white board. Always be prepared to draw a model or create a flow chart of your view of the world and ask the executive to comment about his or her organization.
- Utilize techniques such as "lunch and learns" that provide the executive and the executive's team a chance to learn some best practices and check you out for the price of an hour's time and a cold ham sandwich. At the same time, you have the opportunity to learn about executive issues and start building relationships.

The Fifth Commandment: Coordinate the Selling Team

Ponder Point: The synergy of many driving with a common fate and shared destiny is a powerful force for positive change.

Everyone admires star quarterbacks. They are the sales leaders that land the biggest accounts and earn the highest commissions. These unique individuals are highly competent and fluently and effortlessly present both the product and services side of the business to prospects. However, these people are quite rare, and what is frequently not noticed is that successful services selling often requires a "selling team" approach. When one of the authors was with Andersen Consulting (now Accenture), his managing partner had a habit of saying, "Anyone can throw the long bomb and sometimes win the game, but what makes it happen is the basic blocking and tackling that goes on every day." In professional services selling, blocking, and tackling comes about through the effective coordination of the selling team. Defining what roles you require on the team and aligning them with the sales environment are keys to your success.

One model utilized by some of the (former) "Big Five" consulting firms includes three primary roles on the selling team: the rainmaker, the business developer, and the market researcher. Furthermore, our experience has shown that many services organization's sales teams are well served by having a fourth role defined, that of the specialist. This person brings to the team a deep knowledge of a field or technology relevant to the issues of the account. Table VI shows the roles best suited to coordinate the effort and have the desired impact.

Table VI: The Roles of the Selling Team

Team	Expected Impact
Rainmaker	Closes deals, fully understands total solutions selling; has mastered services selling techniques
Business developer	Solid working understanding of the product and services side of business and can communicate strategically at all levels of a relationship; faces the marketplace without fear and believes strongly in the company and its solutions capability; the one who creates a beachhead and opens doors for the closer or technical experts to participate
Market researcher	A data master who assists the team in understanding the prospect's needs, place in the marketplace, and greatest industry challenges; provides input to the team related to trends, best practices, and information on competitors
Specialist	Provides technical insights and credibility to the team

The second ingredient of successful team selling requires aligning the team with the sales environment. In this regard, some simple and straightforward planning is required. Make sure the performance specifications are clear, realistic, and aligned with each other. All of these should support the business strategy as well. Adequate resources, support staff, and appropriate tools help keep the path forward more focused. And ensuring that logical consequences which will support the desired performance because they are particularly meaningful to the performer helps motivation and goal achievement. But most important, use quality feedback that is relevant, accurate, timely, specific, and easy to understand if you want the team to work in unison and with a basis for action.

BEST PRACTICES

- Institute a semiannual account planning system that clearly identifies roles, responsibilities, expectations, and timelines.
- Make each team member personally responsible for building and managing a relationship with his or her client counterpart.
- Change the reward system to award team performance as well as individual performance.
- Conduct cross-account sharing with other teams at least every quarter.

The Sixth Commandment: **Compress the Cycle Time of Selling**

Ponder Point: A fast "no" is better than a slow "yes."

Professional selling is about building relationships, creating trust, and painting intangible concepts so that the prospect feels comfortable enough to move forward. All these components require time, and time is a precious commodity in selling services. So when one reads the directives of traditional selling prose such as: "Strike while the iron is hot!" "Go for the close!" "Embrace resistance statements and turn lemons into lemonade!" an appropriate queasiness in the stomach follows.

Simple admonishments to "go get 'em" aren't nearly enough to close business in complex selling situations. Left alone without a structured business development process, sales opportunities can string out the selling cycle to months or even years.

Furthermore, we are always amazed at the time, effort, and organizational frenzy that often accompany sales efforts that should never have been attempted in the first place. How often have your organization's scarce resources been misspent trying to get projects that, upon analysis, were never within the realm of possibility? Or worse yet, how often have you gotten the business on projects where your company could never profitably meet client expectations?

Tools and processes are required to systematically compress sales cycle times by (1) qualifying good business and (2) using key events to demonstrate account interest.

Qualifying Good Business

At our own firm, we have assisted numerous professional services clients to first define their ideal business, then work through and create a qualifying checklist made up of the specific factors most important to sizing up good business potential. This is a powerful approach to compressing selling cycle time, as you can quickly and objectively compare business opportunities using a common standard of quality. Use the checklist in Table VII to visualize a key account or prospective client you have targeted and assess how qualified they are (Alexander, 2001). We think the results will surprise you.

Keep in mind that the higher your overall score, the better position you will be in to get the business and the shorter the cycle time of the sale. If your overall score is quite low—move on! Focus your limited resources where they will yield the greatest return. Ride a winner and cut a loser short.

Improving the Committing Process Through Understanding Key Events

Additionally, it is quite important to fully understand what the key events are in moving a prospective client through the committing process. What we mean by this is that you must understand ahead of time the important actions that you need the

Table VII: The Qualifying Checklist

Success Factors	Rating				
	low				high
1. Importance to the account	1	2	3	4	5
2. Business fit	1	2	3	4	5
3. Personal fit	1	2	3	4	5
4. Our reputation with account	1	2	3	4	5
5. Account partnership attitude	1	2	3	4	5
6. Competitive position	1	2	3	4	5
7. Access to the decision makers	1	2	3	4	5
8. Funding	1	2	3	4	5
9. Importance to us	1	2	3	4	5
10. Timing	1	2	3	4	5
TOTAL SCORE =					

Source: Adapted from Alexander and Lyons, 1995.

prospect to take to accelerate the buying decision. Remember that buyer motivation usually is based on two things: confidence and urgency. Building this confidence and creating a sense of urgency can be a challenge, but if you follow the following four-step process, then the task will gain its own sense of momentum:

1. *Envision the ideal.* Create in your mind's eye what an ideal process looks like from the time you first meet the account through the time you close the deal. How will you position yourself and your company? How will you match the prospect's personality? How will you establish rapport? What will your opening statement be? How will you demonstrate your knowledge and understanding of his or her service challenges? How will you illustrate your capability and involve the client in the proposed solution (Hordes, 2001)?

2. *Map your existing process.* Take time before a sales call to map out what each step is in how you will approach the sales process. In most circumstances, no more than four steps will

be in the process. Get feedback from others on your sales team about whether these steps make sense and use that feedback to explore ways to streamline and refine the process.

3. *Create the new process.* Think of the sales process from a new perspective. Ask yourself: If we had a clean sheet of paper and this was day 1 of the company, how would we do it differently? What existing steps would we eliminate? What barriers would be removed? What support would be enhanced? What best practices would be included? How could it be done so that the cycle time and overall impact would create the greatest effect and at the same time reduce the risk of rejection by the prospect?

4. *Implement.* Execution is always important, so make sure you have the appropriate alignment of your sales organization in place with the appropriate supports and resources to make it happen.

BEST PRACTICES

• Conduct a focus group to discover your organization's true sales cycle time. Pick the participants' brains to uncover the key events that most consistently either advance sales or get in the way.

• Have a "Go/No-Go" checklist already established. Take the findings from your information gathering to decide whether this business should be pursued.

• Allocate resources to prospective accounts according to their probability of success.

The Seventh Commandment: **Concentrate on the Stars**

Ponder Point: The performance improvement potential of most sales forces is 700%. No kidding.

Sales management has a basic choice when it comes to the development of its sales force: Focus efforts on the low, average, or top performers. If you examine the majority of sales organizations you'll find the following:

- The training budget is geared toward the new and average performers with a focus on "blocking and tackling" skills.
- Sales management's one-on-one coaching efforts are almost entirely dedicated to the low-performing, problem children—those a long way from meeting quota.
- The stars are left alone. (Hey, they're doing great, so why bother?)

So to sum it up, most effort is spent on the low performers, and most resources (training) are targeted toward average performance, with little, if anything, targeted for the old pros.

The logic seems reasonable, yet this is a formula for mediocrity. Under this scenario, resources are devoted to reinforce "average" performance. No organization can make dramatic strides ahead focusing on the status quo. The results prove this—how many services organizations routinely increase revenues more than 10% per year?

Let us suggest an alternative that we strongly feel can have an immediate and profound effect. In fact, for organizations currently under the above regime that commit to the steps we outline, the sales productivity of your services organization should improve 25% or more within one year.

Over twenty years ago, one of the founders of the field of performance technology, Thomas Gilbert, came up with the simple yet powerful formula for computing a function's performance improvement potential (PIP) (Gilbert, 1978). He stated that his usual finding in working with organizations of all types was that the sales function was the area that showed the greatest performance opportunity. The usual sales PIP was about a 7, meaning the opportunity was present to increase revenue seven times more than what it was currently.

Here is an example of calculating the PIP for a professional services sales force that sells $19,250,000 per year (see Figure 35 for a visual representation):

1. *Identify "star" performance.* In this sales force of twenty, the top salesperson sold at a rate of $5 million of professional services per year.

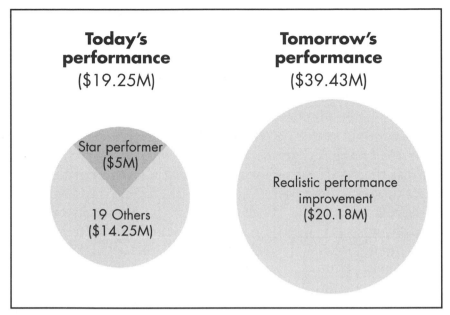

Today's performance
($19.25M)

Star performer
($5M)

19 Others
($14.25M)

Tomorrow's performance
($39.43M)

Realistic performance
improvement
($20.18M)

Figure 35: The sales improvement potential.

2. *Identify "average" performance.* The remaining nineteen salespeople sold on average $750 thousand of professional services per year (for a total of $14.25 million). The left-hand side of Figure 35 shows visually this current state of sales.

3. *Determine the maximum performance improvement potential.* So this sales force had a PIP of 6.6 ($5,000,000 /$750,000), meaning that the star salesperson was 6.6 times more effective in selling than the average.

   If it were possible to get everyone to perform at the level of the star performer, annual revenues would go from $19,250,000 to $100,000,000—a potential increase in revenue dollars of $80,750,000.

4. *Establish a "realistic" PIP.* Differences in the sales environment (number and type of accounts, market conditions, etc.) do have a bearing and cannot be ignored. Furthermore, of those nineteen "non-star" performers, one or two might have been new to the sales force and thus have had less

experience, which should be considered. Therefore, to be conservative, calculate a "realistic PIP" by determining one-fourth of the total PIP.

The right-hand side of Figure 35 shows the realistic performance improvement potential of the sales force in the example is $20,187,500, double the existing revenue.

Who would not be delighted with doubling existing revenue? The good news is that this is doable. Gilbert's research reported that the very best performers do just a few things different from the rest of the pack (Gilbert, 1978). In most cases, skilled observers can define those behaviors in a matter of days. Usually, what is learned can readily be taught to the rest of the sales organization with awesome results. This is truly an area of low-hanging fruit.

So our recommendations are to dramatically change your focus on sales force development. Put your time and money in the place that will yield the greatest return on investment (ROI), your top performers, and use their results and behaviors as the targets and models for everyone else. The laggards will "de-select" themselves, and the average performers will step up to the challenge.

Best Practices

- Conduct a yearly "star analysis," and use it as the framework for establishing PIPs, determining critical sales behaviors, and creating hiring profiles for future recruits. Train everyone who comes into contact with customers on what you have learned from this process.
- Reformulate your sales development plan to spend:
  - 40% of the time working with your very best. Observe and question to find out their secrets.
  - 50% of your time observing your average performers. Teach them what you've learned from the best.
  - Only 10% of your time working with the laggards. Yes, they deserve a chance to improve, but this is almost always a system issue and not a coaching problem.

- Make sure your sales management system is performance-based, not activity-based.
- Make managers personally accountable for the recruitment, development, and retention of top performers.
- Dole out substantial incentives for employees that induce top outsiders to join your sales team.
- Tolerate unusual behavior from the stars. Often their success lies in going around the existing system and snubbing the accepted norms of behavior.
- Form a partnership with a professional-services-savvy search firm.
- Create alumni networks to maintain relationships with key personnel.
- Encourage your stars to write and speak.
- Encourage and reward stars for mentoring new salespeople.
- After two or three years, conduct a star-performer analysis of a top-flight sales organization outside your industry.

The Eighth Commandment: **Control the Cost of Sales**
Ponder Point: There is nothing more wasteful and expensive than doing something extremely well that should never have been done in the first place.

Controlling the cost of sales requires the formulation of four basic budgets: the sales budget, the selling expense budget, the advertising and marketing budget, and the sales administration budget. All four of these components must work in an integrated process in order to adequately forecast revenue, margin, utilization, and expense. Proper potential-customer segmentation as well as targeting high-potential clients and legacy customers with a weighting system is one approach. The strategy, as well as the budget, is quite different when your target is to leverage an existing account where you already have a relationship versus going after a segment of the services marketplace in which you are not the dominant leader.

Sometimes you have to invest in order to save, and this is very true in looking at the economics of sales force management. For example, a friend of ours dedicated to improving the capabilities of his sales organization was getting some resistance from people in the organization about taking the salespeople out of the field for three days of training. We very much believe in his response: "If you think the cost and time for training is expensive, try ignorance!" A rather interesting perspective on reducing the overall cost of the sales process, don't you think?

Although important, trying to maintain an ongoing focus on reducing the cost of sales is not always easy, as the excitement and perceived urgency of getting in front of any and all prospects in person is often in direct conflict with cost control. Sometimes the most effective way to think about controlling the cost of sales is based upon what not to do:

- Don't call on low-qualified accounts, ever!
- Don't make a face-to-face visit if a phone call will do.
- Don't make a phone call if an e-mail is sufficient.
- Don't send an e-mail if the prospect, customer, or client can get necessary information or take the desired action via the Web.
- Don't ask your support people to do tasks that can be automated or can be made into customer self-service via the Web.
- Don't take your Web page for granted and assume that what you have on it is of interest to anyone other than yourself. Keep it updated and relevant to customer needs.

BEST PRACTICES
- Track the cost of sales.
- Support the planning for sales calls in different regions by telemarketing and electronic sales materials.
- Link individual face-to-face meetings with prospects to conferences and briefing sessions on critical strategic business issues.
- Deploy ample marketing budgets to support the development of case studies, white papers, and thought-leadership publications.

- Keep collateral materials in modules, enabling a high degree of flexibility for adjustments in the sales call process.
- Keep the proposal process highly systematized through the utilization of support technology such as Lotus Notes, group collaboration tools, and PSA/CRM software. By doing this, a proposal, which normally would cost $25,000 to produce, can be developed in half the time and at half the cost.
- Qualify all prospects using a standard qualifying checklist (see the Sixth Commandment).
- Train everyone that comes in contact with customers on appropriate selling tools and techniques.
- Allow sales personnel to sell and not get bogged down in administrative duties that a $30-an-hour support person can carry out.
- See that selling support systems (knowledge management, promotional materials, etc.) are in place and are utilized throughout the organization.
- Reward the sales team on profitability.

The Ninth Commandment: Commercialize the Sales Promise

Ponder Point: No matter how superior your solution, you are ten times more likely to get the business if the prospect calls you rather than if you call the prospect.

Chapter 4 emphasized the power of your organization's credibility factor and the door-opening power of a strong brand. Nothing in selling is better than having the prospect call you. Commercializing the sales promise means maximizing your marketing efforts by making sure that the selling function delivers on the value proposition promised by your branding efforts.

BEST PRACTICES

- Make sure the entire sales organization understands the organization's services value proposition, its market message, and the services strategy that drives them.

- Train everyone who comes in contact with customers to communicate the services value proposition within a common framework.
- See that all sales "packaging" (people, communications, pricing, physical environment) convey the same consistent market message.

The Tenth Commandment: **Continually Learn and Grow**

Ponder Point: "...the rate at which individuals and organizations learn may be the only sustainable competitive advantage."
–Ray Stata, CEO, Analog Devices

Earlier in our careers, we were intrigued by the concept of a learning organization. We remember that, during that time, it was a wonderful thought that learning and professional growth were not only lifetime experiences but that corporate America was building systems and designing organizations to embrace these values. The need for the learning organization has proven to be valid, as industry after industry has undergone dramatic change, requiring not only a rethinking of business models but a retooling of knowledge and skills.

Those of us involved in professional services over the last ten years have witnessed the enormous growth of the number of once-staunch product companies making the transition to services-led s-businesses. Today, s-businesses are proving their organizational value and starting to take equal place alongside their product-focused brethren (Alexander and Hordes, 2002a). Some of these companies are building service strategies to pull existing product lines, others are building step-out services, and many have radically reduced their product lines. Some companies like PeopleSoft and IBM have even become services-led and -leveraged.

Yet we have observed the strain this transition creates for both organizational and personal capabilities. These changes require radical departures from the traditional skill sets upon which these businesses were built; hence, the ability to continually learn and grow is more important than ever. And, as has been pointed out throughout this chapter, in no area are the challenge and the importance greater than in selling.

BEST PRACTICES

- Expect that all personnel involved in selling should spend a minimum of two weeks per year in some type of intensive education.
- Make learning opportunities easy by utilizing a variety of approaches, such as on-site workshops, simulations, online training, and public seminars.
- Formalize coaching as a sales management requirement.
- Ask all top performers to mentor new salespeople.
- Commission a culture study to learn about how your organization accepts change.
- Invite speakers outside your industry to discuss best practices on topics such as services marketing or sales effectiveness.
- Create a knowledge-management database of best practices, case studies, and articles.
- Allocate 5% of your gross revenue to continuing education. In the services business, your most valuable assets are your employees' talent and mind share. Invest in them!

To be successful in the new s-business world, the opportunity to continue to grow and learn is essential. Building services competency and capability will require taking a strong stance on allocating resources to train and deploy a services workforce that not only understands the full life cycle of a services sale but can articulate industry trends and market intelligence issues.

Aligning the Selling Approach to the Services Strategy

Except as noted, all of the above commandments have utility no matter what your services organization's situation. This section will tailor that content to the specific ramifications associated with each of the four services strategies. To start with, let's

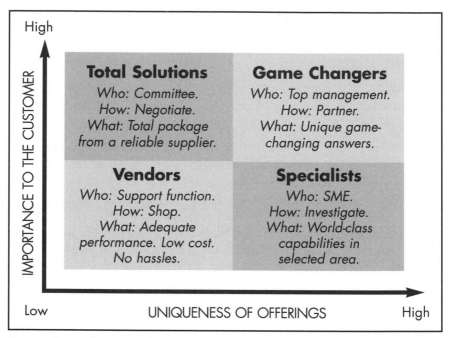

Figure 36: S-business buyers.

review things from the customer's vantage point, as discussed earlier in Chapter 3.

In Figure 36, *Who* refers to the person or persons making the buying decision; *How* refers to the buying strategy usually employed in purchasing a services offering from a particular type of services provider; *What* refers to the value proposition that customers are looking for. Let's consider the selling implications.

Total Solutions

The buyer evaluating a Total Solutions offering is usually a committee headed by a top functional executive looking for a total package from a reliable supplier. Because normally there will be at least two or three organizations offering similar sounding packages, the buying strategy is to negotiate the best deal.

Since the buying committee will include a variety of people with different backgrounds, needs, and expectations, it is most appropriate to have a selling team led by a rainmaker with the team members matched (in terms of knowledge, background, personality) to the members of the buying team. Because of the size and competitiveness of these types of deals, very strong selling capabilities are required to (1) land the deal, (2) not give away the farm in getting the business, and (3) realistically shape expectations. All other things being equal, the quality of the proposal will carry the day. Hence, proposal writing excellence is a requirement, and an excellent selling strategy is to try to shape the specification for the request for proposal (RFP). The most appropriate organizing approach is by account (and possibly by industry). Win ratios and cost of sales are two metrics particularly important to Total Solutions selling.

Game Changers

The top managers who buy from Game Changers are looking for innovative, high-impact answers. Therefore, they will actively partner to address their critical business issues.

These customers prefer to buy from peers, so partners, principals, and senior executives of the game-changing organization are the ones responsible for building relationships and closing deals. Credibility is vital to playing this role so a very strong pedigree coupled with excellent communications skills is vital. Reputations built up over years of demonstrated performance coupled with strong public relations are what bring people to Game Changers. Win ratios and the PR impact of the assignment are two especially important selling metrics.

Specialists

The buyers of specialist services offerings are usually subject matter experts in particular niches. Purchasing is often involved, but the subject matter expert (SME) really sets the specs and makes the decision. The SME is looking for world-class services in this particular niche and will investigate all options to find the right offerings.

Often a mini-selling team (a dedicated industry sales person glued to the hip of a technical services rep) works the best. This selling team is organized by industry (and sometimes by account as well.) Original research reports, case studies, and testimonials help build the services organization's case for being an expert in its field. Because such organizations are Niche players, they need to get all the business in their defined space they can. Therefore, market penetration is a key selling metric.

Vendors

Buyers considering services offerings from Vendors come from support functions (often purchasing) and are looking for adequate performance, low cost, and no hassle. They see the commodities sold by Vendors as solely transactional and not very important, and, hence, they *resent* time wasted talking to salespeople, either face-to-face or over the phone. These buyers prefer to read and compare commodity specifications at their leisure.

So the most appropriate, no hassle selling approach for Vendors is to have no sales force at all! Your marketing efforts must carry the day by using direct mail and advertising with an easy-to-navigate Web site with simple e-commerce capabilities a first priority. Next, a "tag-along" selling strategy should be put in place in which you align with other services providers selling higher-value offerings and they pull your offerings along as a part of their services bundle. In this approach, their sales people become your salespeople. Once "in" with a customer, you have a good chance of staying there, so it makes sense to promote self-renewing contracts. The selling metric most important to Vendors is cost, with a zero cost of sale being the target.

Conclusion

In the majority of s-business organizations, the business development process offers the largest bunch of low hanging fruit. The ten commandments discussed in this chapter help to shape and guide appropriate selling actions for all services selling organizations. However, to be effective, the selling approach must align with the organization's overall services strategy.

Chapter 6

S-Business Delivery:
Turning Customers into Clients

RESEARCH FACTOID: Five of the fourteen best s-practices are delivery-related.

PONDER POINT: No one has more influence on repeat business than the services providers, no one.

PURPOSE: The readers of this chapter will learn:
- Core and best delivery practices of top-performing s-businesses
- The consulting challenge: low client satisfaction
- Expectations, roles, and capabilities of services providers
- The service provider's business development potential impact—low hanging fruit
- The eight universal rules of engagement management
- The engagement management model in action
- Aligning sales with services delivery

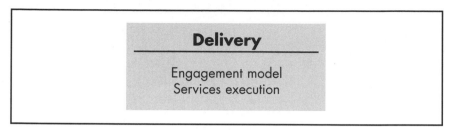

Figure 37: The delivery success lever.

Delivery from an s-business perspective ensures that good (sometimes great) work is consistently performed and executed in a way that is profitable and repeatable. Supported by the appropriate tools, the enablers of sound s-business delivery are engagement management (process) coupled with services execution (people) (Figure 37). This chapter will address both of these elements, starting with the people side of things (the roles and expectations of services providers) and then shifting to the process side (engagement management).

Note: The pattern so far in this book has been to share the core and best practices related to a particular success lever at or near the end of a chapter, as a kind of summary. However, the best practices associated with delivery are a little unique: (1) The overall potential impact to the services organization is large (five of the fourteen best practices from the s-business study [Alexander, 2002] concern delivery), and (2) most of the best delivery practices are actions not normally considered a part of traditional services delivery. Therefore, in this chapter we have decided to start with delivery best practices (summarized in Figure 38) to lend credence to our selected content and emphasis. (For the meaning of single and double asterisks, refer to Figure 38.)

Core and Best Delivery Practices

Best Practices

PROJECT MANAGERS KNOW HOW TO MANAGE PROJECT SCOPE**

Do any of these sound familiar? "I thought that your sales guy said the project included these additional items!" Or: "Oh, by

Project managers:

- Know how to manage project scope.**

Services providers:

- Utilize a common methodology.**
- Demonstrate appropriate selling skills.**
- Possess adequate account management skills.**
- Have access to real-time customer information.**
- Understand the services industry.*
- Understand process consulting.*
- Know the critical business issues of their customers.*

Figure 38: Delivery: best practices.

*   Statistically proven s-business differentiator from product-centered company.
** Statistically proved practice of top-performing s-businesses.

the way, can you help out the accounts-payable folks? I'm out of money, but it should only take a few days. I'd really appreciate it." In every delivery cycle there comes a time when "scope creep" raises its head—the customer requests something that goes beyond the agreed-upon project scope. Effective project managers are well prepared for this phenomenon, with plans in place to deal with it developed early on.

SERVICE PROVIDERS UTILIZE A COMMON METHODOLOGY**.

The best services providers follow the same steps in implementation every time. This approached is codified throughout the organization. Yes, geographic, industry, or services lines may add some special nuances, but by and large the methodology should remain the same across the organization.

SERVICES PROVIDERS DEMONSTRATE APPROPRIATE SELLING SKILLS**

As will be emphasized in this chapter, active business development by services providers can have a huge impact on the performance of the services organization. A few well-placed selling skills can make all the difference.

Services Providers Possess Adequate Account Management Skills**

The best services businesses implement account management practices for key accounts, and the services providers are a part of this approach. They are actively involved in helping to expand penetration across the customer organization.

Services Providers Have Access to Real-Time Customer Information**

In the top-performing s-businesses, services providers are able to get up-to-date customer data any time, any place. This allows not only for greater responsiveness but for compressing cycle times.

Services Providers Understand the Services Industry*

When services technicians and consultants understand how the services business works, they have more credibility with customers. This can be an important differentiator when competitor technical skills are seen as being equivalent.

Services Providers Understand Process Consulting*

The people providing services have a knowledge of the steps to consult and the appropriate actions they should take during each phase of the consulting.

Services Providers Know the Critical Business Issues of Their Customers*

Services providers that understand customers and their most important challenges and opportunities build more trust than those that don't.

Consulting Delivery

Because the majority of the above practices deal directly with the capabilities of the services provider, that is where we will start.

Note: We recognize that the roles and responsibilities of services providers can vary greatly. For example, the situation a services technician finds himself/herself in responding to a frantic call to get a system back up can be quite different from the reality of a consultant officing at a client location during a ten-month engagement. However, our premise is that the *core* issues, expectations, needs, wants, and requirements are basically the same across *all* types of services providers and that all services providers would benefit by striving to achieve the attributes of the consultant that we will describe. For that reason and for the sake or simplicity, we will only use the terminology and examples most associated with "consulting" delivery.

The Consulting Challenge

No matter how the services organization keeps score, it is ultimately the degree of customer acceptance-satisfaction-delight that determines repeat business and future profitability. Hence, the information shown in Figure 39 is a little disturbing (Kennedy Information Research Group, 1999).

As you'll note in Figure 39, for each type of consultant, satisfaction scores ranged from a low of 3.40 out of 5 for information technology (IT) personnel to 3.85 out of 5 for human resources (HR) personnel. In customer satisfaction research, customers that provide scores below 3.5 are very susceptible to changing service providers and anything under 4.0 is considered vulnerable. On the other side of the spectrum, it takes very high levels of customer satisfaction (4.7+ depending upon whose research you believe) to generate customer loyalty. Based upon the scores shown, services organizations should be pretty concerned. It is our feeling that how services are sold has a big impact downstream on customer satisfaction. Nevertheless, it is the delivery team's responsibility to deliver on expectations whatever the situation, and these metrics question their effectiveness. On the other hand, these low-performance scores demonstrate a big opportunity for those organizations willing to step up and address the gap. How do your satisfaction scores stack up? (For a not so amusing story on the consequences of not understanding a client's expectations adequately, see the sidebar "Duh! It's All About Value.")

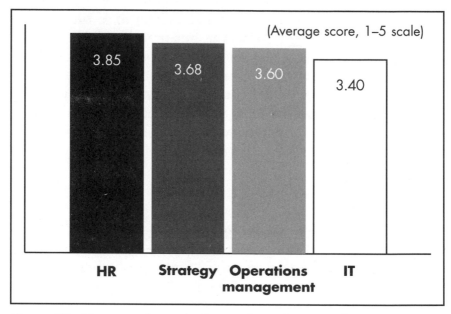

Figure 39: The consulting challenge: low client satisfaction.
Source: Kennedy Information Research Group, 1999.

Client Expectations of Consultants

In earlier work conducted by one of the authors, client expectations of consultants were determined. Figure 40 lists the eight most commonly heard expectations ranked by importance. Thinking again about the satisfaction scores discussed

Figure 40: Client expectations of consultants.

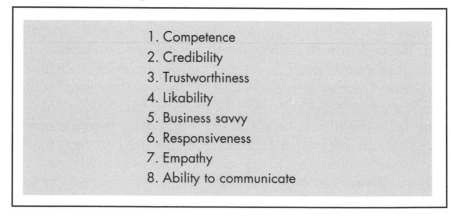

above, one possible reason for the low scores might be a difference in perception of what clients expect and what consultants think clients expect. When working on improving consultant effectiveness, we routinely ask groups of consultants to rank the highest-priority expectations of clients. In almost every case,

Duh! It's All About Value

"Worry about the crop, not the plow" (Gilbert, 1978). A simple example can prove the point. Many years ago in a different life, one of the authors was responsible for a team of 100 consultants delivering a large SAP project to a resources client. Dutifully each week, every consultant reported what he/she did and the hours it took. After about three months into the engagement, the client started a process in which the entire client management team would meet weekly to discuss project performance. Their discussion was played through a loudspeaker so that the entire delivery team could be apprised of the meeting.

The meetings went something like this: "John Smith—what value did he deliver this week?" None! Drop him from the project! "Mary Jones—what about her?" Partial value. OK, let her stay! "Bill Blue? No value there! Take him off as well!" Well, in a matter of two more months, no one was left on the project and it all came crashing down around our heads. Despite our best efforts and our honest approach to meet project objectives, we were not successful.

The biggest lesson learned from that experience was that clients don't really care about what you've done, they are only interested in positive results of what you've done. Your project status reports may require listing traditional items such as task, completion dates, and time allocation, but do yourself a favor: Add one more column called Value Delivered or Client Impact and start your client conversations addressing what the client finds important.

there are major differences. Figure 41 shows the base client expectations listed earlier with an example of the what consultants think. You'll notice some important differences in perception.

The Traditional Consultant Role

With client expectations defined, it is time to take a look at the traditional role of the services provider, in this case the consultant.

The consultant's traditional role (Figure 42) is limited to the fourth and final sub-process of the business development process introduced in Chapter 5. Within those parameters, consultants strive to do their part in turning customers into clients by first of all consistently delivering value. This means helping the project manager bring in the project up to quality, on time, and within budget. It also entails the very important task of setting, managing, and meeting client expectations at the same time. In special situations designated by the client, consultants also need to have the ability to greatly exceed client expectations. Also, effective consultants should be empowered, skilled, and motivated to immediately and without management input implement service recovery steps when big project problems occur. Finally, in their traditional role, good consultants should

Figure 41: Client expectations of consultants compared with what consultants thought.

Clients said...	Consultants thought...
1. Competence.	1. Results.
2. Credibility.	2. Reliability.
3. Trustworthiness.	3. Confidence.
4. Likability.	4. Credibility.
5. Business savvy.	5. Empathy.
6. Responsiveness.	6. Responsiveness.
7. Empathy.	7. Hired help.
8. Ability to communicate.	

CUSTOMERS   CLIENTS

1. Consistently deliver value by:
   - Bringing in projects up to quality, on time, and within budget.
   - Setting, managing and meeting client expectations.
2. Occasionally (when planned) greatly exceed client expectations.
3. Immediately implement "service recovery" when a project goes south.
4. Respond enthusiastically when asked about your organization's capabilities.

Figure 42: The consultant's traditional role.

be able to quickly, accurately, and enthusiastically reply to questions about their services organization and its capabilities.

These are all vital responsibilities and often not easy to perform well. In fact, many leaders would be phenomenally grateful to have the majority of their consultants fulfilling the traditional role requirements. Training, coaching, and performance tools along with strong business processes are needed to help consultants meet these standards. However, we contend that these actions are not nearly enough. They are just the building blocks upon which to construct a more formidable structure.

The High-Impact Consultant Role

Let's go back to the complete business development process for a minute. When we think things through, we realize that consultants have the potential to impact *all* aspects of business development. Who else is in a better position to learn of new client

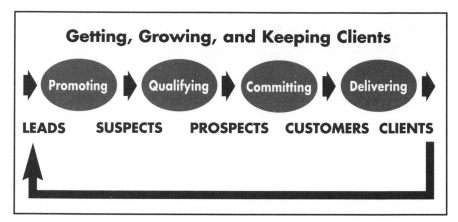

Figure 43: The consultant's zone of influence.

opportunities than a consultant on the ground at the client's site working day after day with his or her client counterparts? Who else should be more trusted than the professional who has already proven his/her technical capability and ability to get things done? In the majority of cases, clients will be much more willing to talk about their wishes and wants with consultants than with those in a more formal selling role. Furthermore, it is not unusual for the ratio of people tasked solely with business development to those in a consulting role to be 1:100—which means, with a few minor adaptations, the ability to expand the selling force 100-fold! What a great example of low-hanging fruit: tapping the awesome business development potential of consultants. Figure 43 shows the consultant's zone of influence. Figure 44 shows our recommended role of the consultant—one that not only delivers today's business but plays an integral role in creating tomorrow's.

Note: This potential crosses all services strategies. The role outlined below is equally important to services providers pursuing a Mean and Lean strategy as to those attempting to be Game Changers.

What does it take to get the majority of consultants willing and able to assume this expanded role? Surprisingly, not a lot. Here are the few required steps:

> **Help generate new business by:**
> 1. Listening and probing for client issues
> 2. Qualifying client opportunities
> 3. Passing the qualified opportunity on to the appropriate person
>   or by
>   Closing the business himself or herself

Figure 44: Recommended high-impact consultant's role.

1. Explain the benefit of embracing this new consultant role to clients, consulting organizations, and the consultants themselves. Once consultants understand that professional selling adds value to clients and that clients *want* their input, most of the resistance goes away.
2. Create new business develop objectives for consultants, along with highly visible methods of recognition and healthy rewards for accomplishing goals and some consequences for not meeting them.
3. Provide some quality, consultant-specific training on business development. A day or two of imparting knowledge and building skills (supported by tools) will create not only adequate competence but enough confidence to generate new behaviors with clients.

Ponder Point: What a huge potential return for a very modest investment.

The Four Consulting Capabilities

We have identified client expectations, and talked about the new consultant role we recommend, so now it is time to take a look at the consultant from a capabilities standpoint. Figure 45 shows the four consulting capabilities. Technical expertise is assumed, as it would be difficult to be a consultant if one did not possess a level of deep expertise in some field. Of course, technical expertise varies according to your services offerings. To clients, it is a given and they expect it walking in the door.

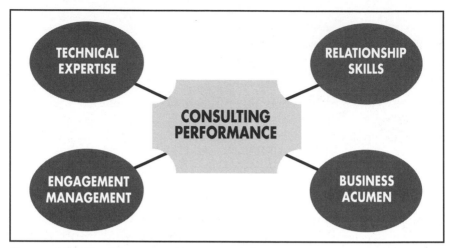

Figure 45: The four consulting capabilities.

Engagement management, the topic of our next section, means that all consultants understand the company's process and can capably navigate its course. All organizations need a common, efficient methodology here, with everyone who comes into contact with customers well versed in its implementation.

The two areas of consultant capability building that are frequently not formally addressed by services organizations are business acumen and client relationship skills. In debriefing accounts when you didn't get the business, one of the most common complaints you'll hear is that the consultants (and other members of the team) didn't appear to understand the account's business. The significance of this lack of business acumen becomes more and more important the higher up in the potential client's organization the individuals are that the consultant must deal with. Although not really important at Vendor level, business acumen is definitely important at Specialist level and vital at Game Changer and Total Solutions Provider levels.

At other times you may receive feedback (possibly similar to the client satisfaction scores noted earlier) at the completion of a project that the client wasn't satisfied with the consultant. What you'll often hear as the reason for the dissatisfaction after some probing is that the consultant "didn't keep me informed," "never seemed to understand where I was coming from," or "didn't' seem to care." These are hard words to swallow since, at its most basic level, consulting is a relationship business. So what it all comes down to is that good relationship skills are what separate adequate consultants from great consultants. Building rapport and trust through consistent, reliable actions creates relationships. Crisply stating what's been done, why it's been done, and the benefit the action will deliver are the core elements of communicating value. Taking the time to think about the situation as if you were in the client's shoes and intelligently probing to learn about the client's problems show concern. Solving current client problems with integrity helps to gain the client's commitment to your solving new problems in the future.

The Relationship Continuum

How well the four consulting capabilities are operationalized (particularly relationship skills) goes a long way toward establishing the consultant's position with a particular client. Table VIII shows a Relationship Continuum along with some dimensions to demonstrate differences. On the left, the consultant is seen as just "another pair of hands" while on the right, the consultant is seen as a "trusted advisor."

When the consultant is viewed as another pair of hands, the client calls all the shots and the consultant sees himself or herself as totally subservient. The particular project is viewed by both parties as just another transaction to be conducted, and both realize that it could well be one of the first to be cut when budgets get scrutinized. When project problems materialize, things often get confrontational and both parties try to look out for themselves through negotiation. If that is not successful, a lawyer enters the fray. The strain of confrontation can be felt throughout the project as the consultant continues to do what he or she deems most important while the client tries to shorten the consultant's involvement and get the job done cheap. Not the most pleasant relationship.

On the other side of the spectrum is an entirely different reality. When the client sees the consultant as a trusted advisor, project decisions are made jointly and collaboratively. Both parties view the project as a business relationship and hopefully deem it important enough to be considered a strategic initiative. When problems arise (as they do in even the best working relationships), client and consultant sit down and collaborate together to work things through. In those rare cases in which further intervention is required, they both return to the table to openly talk with the guidance of a non-binding mediator. Both the consultant and the client are focused on one and the same thing—creating worth.

The bottom line is that when you position yourself and your consulting team as "trusted advisors" rather than just "another pair of hands," all kinds of positive things flow from that experience. Delivery is never easy and things you had anticipated don't always fall into line due to organizational changes, shifting of priorities, or faulty contracting with the client. But starting out the relationship as a "trusted advisor" of the client creates more of a shared responsibility type of process which is more likely to produce a worthwhile outcome and mutual satisfaction.

The Eight Universal Rules of Engagement Management

In working with clients in the delivery of professional services, it is imperative that you have a process that outlines how the

Table VIII: The Relationship Continuum

Dimension	Another pair of hands	Trusted advisor
Decision making	100% Client calls the shots	50-50 Collaboration
View of project	Transaction	Business relationship
Project priority	First to be cut	Strategic initiative
Problems arise?	Negotiate/litigate	Collaborate/mediate
Consultant focus	Being billable	Creating worth
Client focus	Get job done cheap	Creating worth

work should be carried out from inception through final completion. It is insufficient to simply state, "The work is done when the client runs out of money!" This process requires eight universal rules of engagement management that need to be followed in order to be successful (Figure 46).

Rules

RULE 1: MAINTAIN CONSISTENCY

The ideal is to identify and appoint a central contact professional who will serve as a liaison to the client. This individual provides not only continuity and consistency to the client over time, but also is the main communication link that handles aspects of planning, scheduling, and the management perhaps of multiple engagements.

RULE 2: HAVE A PROCESS-DRIVEN APPROACH

Understanding where to go with things is a universal business precept. Professionals who are delivering services need to be well grounded in understanding all of the process steps—promoting, qualifying, committing, and delivering services. Many a client-failed project can be tracked back to the consultants who didn't follow a consistent process throughout the engagement. Having a base-line engagement process model provides everyone, including the client, with a level playing field.

Figure 46: The eight universal rules of engagement management.

1. Maintain consistency.
2. Have a process-driven approach.
3. Be clear as to ownership.
4. Utilize performance tools.
5. Integrate quality controls.
6. Use a knowledge management system.
7. Commit *everyone* to obtaining new business.
8. Implement effective and efficient project management.

RULE 3: BE CLEAR AS TO OWNERSHIP

Knowing who has what role at the various levels of a client relationship is a key component of engagement management. Having a clear sense of who "owns" what parts of the engagement is important. Within this context, consider three specific roles:

1. The overall Client Relationship Manager who maintains the long-term perspective and global management of the account
2. The specific Project Manager who oversees a single project with a client to ensure that the work is carried out according to plan and agree-upon expectations
3. The designated Consultant or Consultants, who make up the "brain trust" that helps solve client problems and builds relationships everyday on the job

RULE 4: UTILIZE PERFORMANCE TOOLS

Properly designed performance tools improve the quality of work. Everyone on an engagement needs access to tools, templates, and checklists to maintain the quality of the project as well as to speed it to its completion. Below are *twenty specific tools* that should be part of your overall engagement process:

1. Account Planning Template
2. Qualifying Client Checklist
3. Proposal Template
4. Change Impact Assessment Template
5. Joint Responsibility Matrix
6. Risk Analysis Form
7. Issues Management Log
8. Client Expectations Matrix
9. Project Launch Checklist
10. Project Management Tool Kit
11. Project Status Reporting Form
12. Staffing Skills Matrix

13. Client Relationship Map
14. Progress Meeting Template
15. Project's Integration Template
16. Quality Review Checklist
17. Project Wrap-Up Checklist
18. Account Expansion Map
19. Client and Team Evaluation Form
20. Knowledge Management Engagement Lessons Learned Form

RULE 5: INTEGRATE QUALITY CONTROLS

By this time, most organizations have a quality process, be it the Malcolm Baldrige Quality Framework, Deming, Juran, SPQC, or some home-grown hybrid system. The bottom line is that it is difficult to preach quality of delivery if you don't have a process yourself that everyone follows. Having an initial quality plan as part of the initial engagement management process ensures that problems are identified early and resolved in a manner that is consistent with defect-free work, prevention, and continuous improvement—"The Three Pillars of Quality."

RULE 6: USE A KNOWLEDGE MANAGEMENT SYSTEM

Without exception, if you do not have a knowledge management system for your professional services organization you are headed for trouble. Knowledge workers need information that is easy to obtain and user friendly. In an effective knowledge management system, all relevant information is captured and available anywhere, anytime, by anyone who needs to know.

Your professional services knowledge management systems should include: best practices, tasks packages, methodologies, case studies, project lesson learned, tools, templates, checklists, process maps, industry and client data, client profiles, and executive bio's, to name a few.

RULE 7: COMMIT *EVERYONE* TO OBTAINING NEW BUSINESS

In the world of engagement management, everyone including

the technical folks contributes to getting new, "good" business. All consultants and support staff should have had some level of business development skills training. Everyone should be able to state a "thirty-second" value proposition speech on the elevator with a "C"-level client. Everyone should fully understand all of your service offerings, be capable of asking the right qualifying questions, and be more than "dangerous" when it comes to proactively attracting new good business. An example will drive the point home.

In a three-month project, Max the consultant did exactly as he was told and contributed to getting the systems integrated on time, up to quality, and within budget. Making friends with his client counterpart during the engagement, Max learned that two other larger divisions of the company were facing similar challenges to the one they were working on. Max never asked his friend for more information, never mentioned the opportunity in a project meeting, and didn't e-mail anyone about the opportunity—that was not his job. These projects (and several hundred thousand dollars of revenue) went to a competitor. No one else in Max's services business learned of the projects, and a couple of possible easy sales were lost. Sound familiar?

RULE 8: IMPLEMENT EFFECTIVE AND EFFICIENT PROJECT MANAGEMENT

Much has been written over the years as to what is meant by project management. So a rehash of all the tools, processes, and steps serves little purpose. However, there are four key success elements that are often overlooked in services projects that bear mentioning. These include the following:

1. A dedicated project manager and dedicated project management team is in place.
2. The project manager selects the project team.
3. All projects have a clear beginning and end, with performance milestones along the way.
4. People who will deliver the project are part of the committing process.

Implementing the Rules

The universal rules of engagement ideally should be framed against known best practices that support the project management process: scope, creation of a common methodology, appropriate selling skills, account management capabilities, knowledge of the services industry, knowledge of the business issues of the client, and an understanding of process consulting. Spending time educating your employees about these skills and capabilities is worth your time and effort.

The Engagement Management Process

To this point we have addressed the people side of delivery, outlining expectations, roles, and responsibilities. We have also outlined the process side of things by describing the universal laws of engagement management. This section will attempt to bring this information to life by providing an example of an actual engagement management process used by one of our clients.

The engagement management process is broken into four main phases, each aligning with a sub-process from the business development process: promoting, qualifying, committing, and delivering.

As you'll recall, the promoting process (Figure 47) is all about turning leads into prospects. As the figure shows, whether involving an active, inactive, or prospective client, or a face-to-face, over-the-phone, or over-the-Internet situation, it is everyone's responsibility to seek out potential new business. Therefore, while concurrently working to achieve project objectives, everyone in the services organization should always be listening and probing for client issues. You'll note that a tool, the "Client Issues Worksheet," is provided to help members of the consulting team better understand client issues. Only issues that can be addressed by current services offerings are called *opportunities*, and if they don't meet that criteria they are noted in the CRM as part of the client history. However, if an issue can potentially be positively addressed by the offerings of the consultant's

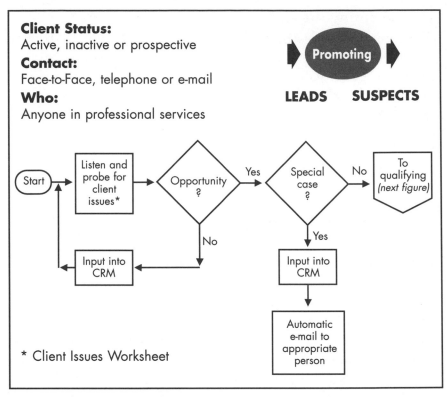

Figure 47: The engagement management process: promoting.

organization, it has passed the first hurdle. The next decision point is whether it's a special case—if it is, then again it is noted into the CRM and an automatic e-mail goes to the appropriate person. If it is not a special case, a suspect has been identified and it is off to the qualifying process.

If you think through your personal experiences, you'll note that in most cases only a very few minutes have been invested up to this point.

Figure 48 looks at the part of the engagement management process that identifies if suspects are also prospects—if they have "good business" potential. Using the Qualifying Checklist (introduced in Chapter 5), the services provider goes down the ten factors and gives each a score based upon his/her knowledge of the client and the situation. If there's not enough informa-

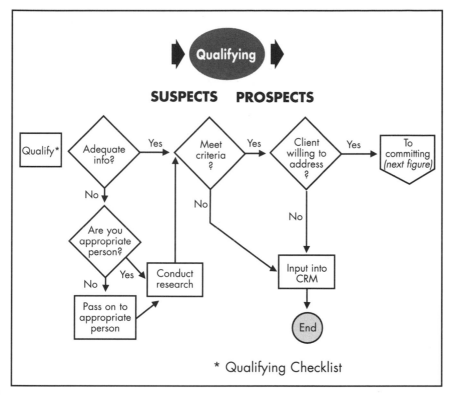

Figure 48: The engagement management process: qualifying.

tion, he/she either passes off to someone else or does some more research until he/she can score each qualifying success factor confidently. If it meets the services organization's criteria (in this case a score of 35 or more out of 50), he/she then confirms that the client is willing to address the identified issue. If it doesn't, the fact is duly noted again in the CRM, and it is back to listening and probing. If the client is open to action, we have a prospect and it is time to move on.

Now it is time for another decision: committing (Figure 49). Broadly speaking, our client has two types of consulting business: "onesy twosys," which are simple, straightforward consulting assignments lasting a day or two. For these situations, consultants are tasked to present a recommendation themselves on the spot. If the client doesn't accept the recommendation,

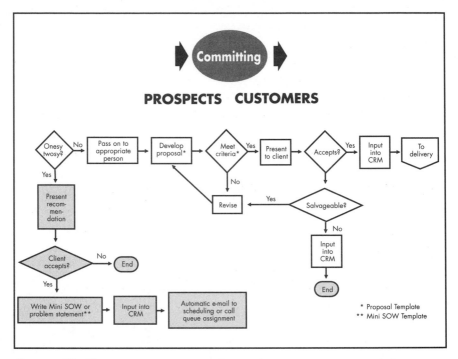

Figure 49: The engagement management process: committing.

the process is ended. If the client accepts, then the consultant writes a brief SOW *(statement of work)* and inputs the information into the CRM, and this "mini project" automatically goes to scheduling. If the consulting potential is more complex, however, our client wants the consultant to hand the project off to a relationship manager. Using another tool, a Proposal Template, this person develops the proposal and passes it on to a quality manager to make sure it meets proposal quality standards. If it does, it goes on to the client; if it doesn't, it is revised until standards are met. If the client doesn't accept, another decision must be made: Is the proposal salvageable? If it isn't, the client is thanked, the scenario is recorded into the CRM, and the action is terminated. If it is salvageable, it is revised and goes back through the proposal loop just described. If and when our client's client accepts the proposal, our client is finally ready to go on to the delivery process (Figure 50).

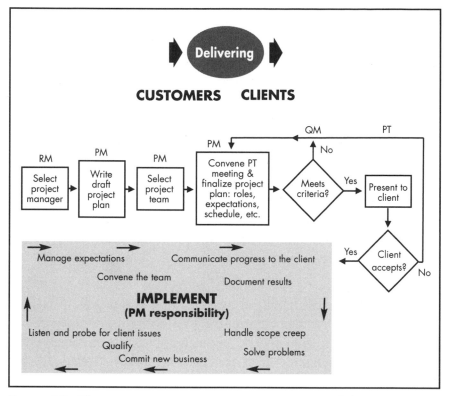

Figure 50: The engagement management process: delivering.

Ideally, the relationship manager (RM) selects the project manager (PM) most appropriate to lead the delivery of the new services offering. At that point, the project manager writes a draft project plan with the help of another template. Next, the project manager selects an appropriate project team (PT) (you guessed it—using another tool) and convenes the team to finalize the project plan, complete with roles defined, expectations set, schedules in place, etc. Since services organization implementations rarely affect only one part of the organization, having some set plans ahead of time to address more integrated issues is important. In this regard, the following six sets of questions should be answered by the project team:

1. *Acceptance.* How can we gain acceptance from others who are both directly or indirectly affected by the implementation?

What advantages can we show for the suggested solution we are proposing? How might we best demonstrate these advantages?

2. *Anticipation*. What objections to our solution can we anticipate? How should we respond? What options do we have to adjust or modify the solution?

3. *Assistance*. How can other people or groups help us apply the solution?

4. *Location*. What places or locations are best suited for putting our solutions into practice?

5. *Timing*. How can we take advantage of special times, days, dates, etc., for implementing our solution?

6. *Precautions*. How can we pretest our solution to ensure its effectiveness?

After these questions have been hashed about and answered, our client's quality management (QM) control system kicks in and someone external to the project and account reviews the plan against established criteria. Once approval is received, the entire team meets with the client to review the plan and reach a mutual acceptance. Then, and only then, does project implementation start, with the PM assuming all the responsibilities outlined in the shaded rectangular box shown in Figure 50.

At that time the process starts all over. While delivering on the expectations of the project just sold, everyone involved is listening and probing for the issues that may turn into the next project.

Aligning the Sales and Delivery Processes

The engagement management process just described is based upon the services provider's proactive involvement in business development. However, usually there are one, two, or more parts of the services-providing organization involved in selling. Hence it is vital that everyone be on the same page, aligned toward the same objectives, aware of each other's actions, helping to understand and solve client problems, and not interfering or competing with each other.

Although everyone (hopefully) has the best interests of the client at heart, sometimes when incentives are structured so that all that is important is to close a deal, what is sold is quite different from what is actually delivered. This leaves the delivery arm of the organization quite frustrated and the client rather perturbed. How can you avoid this type of problem and end up with better alignment? A few best practices can easily be put into place that can bring this about:

- Plan quarterly strategy meetings between sales, marketing, and delivery.
- Create delivery and sales teams that fully understand each other's capabilities.
- Cross-train all three groups—sales, marketing, and delivery—in business development skills.
- Meet monthly to discuss both the pipeline and the current approach to closing each sale as well as the delivery approach that will be undertaken when the work is closed.
- Have a tactical plan as to how the sales function will stay involved during the implementation phases of the project.
- Create sales incentives that are tied to successful delivery, not just to the closing of business.
- Pre-review all proposals through a designated group of delivery professionals to ensure that the firm has the capabilities, resources, and business fit to meet the needs of the client.
- Conduct joint lunch-and-learn sessions where each group presents on a particular topic relevant to the sales function and delivery process.
- Design specific performance measures for the sales and delivery functions that emphasize cooperation, coordination, and successful completion.
- Run success stories in the company newsletter, highlighting cooperation and alignment between sales and delivery.

- Provide a formal evaluation processes where each group assesses the other group as to:
  - What we are doing that is working?
  - What we are not doing that would enhance our joint collaborations?
  - How do we see each of our functions? What do we like and dislike about the other groups?
  - How do we think the other groups see us—the things we do well? the things that we don't do well?
  - What are the alternatives for creative business development and aligned delivery?

Aligning the sales and delivery processes is an important internal and external business process that will not only require your focus but the cooperation of many individuals. Keep in mind that there are two things fundamental in motivating people to change—how they are evaluated and how they are paid. Change your evaluation process to include metrics for joint cooperation, collaboration, and successful delivery coupled with incentives to make it all work and you will see a significant difference in not only alignment but higher client satisfaction as well.

Conclusion

Living the high-impact consulting role within a framework of engagement management is what s-business delivery is all about. Successfully done, the results include higher levels of organizational performance, increased client satisfaction, and deeper, long-term relationships.

Chapter 7

S-Business Operations

RESEARCH FACTOID: Utilizing a common project/engagement tracking system is a best practice.

PONDER POINT: Customer loyalty is a much more important measure than customer satisfaction.

PURPOSE: In this chapter we address the three enablers of effective s-business operations: leverage, managing knowledge, and service quality (Figure 51). Taken as a whole, they form an integrated process from which a solid operations foundation can be built. To ensure that you keep focused, it is important to frequently ask the following questions:

- Are all of our costs and expenses in line with our projections?
- Have we invested in the right things and placed our "bets" accordingly?

- Are we leveraging staff to keep profitability and utilization high?
- At the end of the day, did we make money?

Leverage

Leverage addresses how to increase services revenue by structuring your staffing and expanding current engagement work to yield the highest rate of return on your human capital investments. The landscape is filled with services organizations that did not meet leverage projections because they only offered a uniform rate for all their consultants, (e.g., $2,000 a day) regardless of the experience and mixture of expertise on a particular engagement. At a minimum, establish a fee structure that is set at a higher level for your selected "subject matter experts" and "gray hairs" who are the "keepers of wisdom" and the holders of deep experience in your organization. Experience shows that customers will gladly pay a premium to have these folks on the team.

According to David Maister, in *Managing the Professional Services Firm* (Maister, 1993, p. 36): "The appropriate leverage for any practice is determined by one thing, and one thing alone: the nature of the services the practice is engaged in. A practice that specializes in cutting-edge, high client risk ('brain-surgery') work will inevitably need to be staffed with a

Figure 51: The operations success lever.

Operations

Leverage model
Knowledge management
Service quality

high-partner-to-junior ratio: lower level people will not be able to deliver the quality of services required. On the other hand, practices that deal with more procedural 'non-emergency' needs will be inefficient if they do not have high leverage, since high-priced people should not be doing low-value tasks."

This aligns well with the four services strategies introduced in Chapter 3.

To gain a better understanding of services leverage, let's examine how a Total Solutions Provider would approach the concept. A first step would be to establish an initial "beachhead" at the client location composed of your best people. In this instance, a partner, primarily the client relationship partner, should have high visibility over the first sixty days of the engagement. A key manager and at least two consultants and analysts should support this partner. The role of the partner in this model is to build a quick relationship across the organizations in order to assess the leverage probability as well as the next several projects that might follow the current engagement. What typically follows is a bottoms-up approach adding more and more analysts and consultants to the engagement and less and less of the partner in terms of specific time allocation. As most partners play this role, handling several engagements at once, their time at each location becomes less and less as the project proceeds. Consequently, a higher reliance on the manager who is in place begins to take place. It is not unusual in this situation for a particular manager to stay on a project for three to four years. Many a career of a manager in a consulting firm has been made working on only one project where the manager helped grow revenues and build the initial staffing group from three to over a hundred professionals.

A Vendor, on the other hand, would follow a different path to leverage, bearing down in a particular area to gain scale. Your objective here is to obtain the "right of first refusal" on all segments of future work that fall within your "sweet spot." In this regard, the value exchange is an opportunity for the client to receive a discounted fee structure (typically 20% to 25%) of what you would normally charge. The customer also obtains the advantage of having a consistent group of services or technical consultants in place and the ideal assurance that future work will be carried out in a quality manner. This leverage approach provides *four* distinct advantages:

1. You can count on a continual stream of revenue typically over a three-year period of time.
2. Your utilization rates stay high, keeping your team productive and chargeable.
3. You block out competitors who would like to work with the client.
4. You lower the risk ratio for clients due to their comfort level with your people and previous successful work.

Finally, Game Changers and Specialists have a higher proportion of senior people to juniors on engagements since the deep expertise they have sold can only be delivered by top performers.

An interesting leverage approach appropriate to all strategies is to involve the customer in the engagement so as to create stronger bonding and relationship building that will leverage future work.

In the mixed client/consultant approach, the leverage model for all projects is a mixture of client and consulting personnel. At the high end, we have seen a 50-50 division of work between the resources supplied by the client and those of consulting organization. This type of arrangement provides each organization with some unique advantages:

1. Relationships are built quickly and are usually quite sustainable.
2. Knowledge is transferred and ideally utilized for future projects.
3. A "common-fate" and "shared-destiny" mentality is created.

The downside of this type of arrangement is that clients will have to back-fill positions if they allocate 50% to 100% of the resources. Additionally, you may not see an equal distribution of productivity among the teams. The skills of the consultants may be quite different from and are usually higher than those of the client's employees. The resource team from the client side has the edge about knowledge of the functions and process knowledge of the organization, as well as about the politics that make it all come together.

In addition, some problems often occur regarding to the work ethic of the team. Many consulting firms have a very task-oriented work ethic that follows a philosophy of "we do whatever it takes to get the job done." If that means working twenty hours a day, seven days a week, so be it! Client resources, on the other hand, may not be allowed to work overtime and are out the door at 5:00 p.m. sharp. This can sometimes create disharmony among the team members unless you have a change management process in place as well to bring up and discuss these issues over time.

Leverage is an art in that you have to clearly understand your own firm's capabilities, along with the client's work ethic, motivation, and view of the world as it relates to how that organization likes to staff and resource projects. The bottom line is that you should have the capacity and right model to ensure the right mixture of skills, experience, and pricing strategy that supports the right number of right people working on the right projects at the right time. Keep in mind that in an s-business environment creating the appropriate experiences for your staff and realizing good margins (50% or more) are very much dependent on your ability to leverage.

Knowledge Management

"If you think this is expensive, try ignorance!" lamented the CEO of a Singapore-based services company when questioned why it needed to spend $500,000 to create a Knowledge Management System. The CEO was expressing what many services companies are rapidly beginning to understand: Inside their organizational ranks lie, unknown and relatively untapped, a huge amount of resources and knowledge, know-how, case examples, and best practices that are not fully utilized and shared across the organization.

Knowledge management (KM) focuses on how best to manage the intellectual capital of your organization (the primary asset you offer to clients and customers), in order to effectively store, utilize, and share your best practices, methodologies, case studies, lessons learned, and task packages throughout the organization. Regardless of the particular strategy you choose, the necessity of sharing knowledge across your organization is vital to your long-term success.

Service workers, technicians, consultants, and executives alike have long been frustrated by their inability to identify and apply knowledge contained within their organizations. In many instances, "field locations" are carrying out best practices that have won customer praises, but no other location is aware of them. In some cases, technicians have discovered the best way to handle classical "break-fix" situations and are expanding the work to capture Total Solutions new opportunities. Here again, the process of achieving these results is only shared in company meetings or on-site. The search for finding a "better way of doing things" is often beyond the immediate reach or "mouse click" of many services firms. The net result is an endless independent journey of each location or client team continually designing "one-off" solutions to meet each client problem. The ultimate downside of all this is that mistakes and lessons learned are not shared, creating constant rework and resulting in a higher cost of delivery and lost intellectual capital.

Knowledge management includes both explicit information that is reflective of documentation, best practices, manuals, computer files, books, and CD-ROMs, as well as information available in the minds of employees based on their experiences and solutions to problems that they have utilized in the past. Many professionals in services organizations have worked in other services organizations and have first-hand information and knowledge as to the best practices their former employers use. Many of these companies are now the competitors of the professionals' current companies and from a pure market intelligence perspective this information would be helpful to their current companies. It has been our experience that much of this knowledge could be easily captured by running periodic focus groups with employees to tap into this knowledge as a sharing experience.

In order to understand knowledge management in an s-business environment, we should get our arms around exactly what knowledge is and how it can be deployed in the services industry.

Knowledge is an intellectual asset derived from experience and insights. As a company's most important asset, it should be the organization's primary competitive advantage vehicle. As such, knowledge exists within a company in many varied forms:

- Insights from and about customers
- Tested best practices
- Experiences and lessons learned
- Process task packages
- Information on competitors
- Service models and methodologies
- Contracts and Service Level Agreements.

Knowledge management is:

- Collecting a company's intellectual capital
- Providing the right knowledge to the right people at the right time so that they can utilize "point-of-need" information for rapid decision-making and client solution sets

Knowledge management also has a predicable life cycle as information is captured, shared, learned, improved on, and re-created. All of which leads to improved business results and more effective and efficient operations and delivery.

As professional services firms and product companies move more aggressively into providing services, several factors relating to knowledge come into play:

- Field and consultant mobility and retention make knowledge more vital and at the same time more difficult to acquire. With the current emphasis on both shared services and decentralization occurring in many services companies, the requirement of people throughout the organization to have access to knowledge becomes even more important.

- On the other hand, the amount of information each person can assimilate before reaching overload is a factor to consider. The metaphor that best captures this situation is a "sponge" that can hold a lot of water under normal circumstances. When the input is excessive, the saturation point breaks and the water simply pours through with no retention. The lesson from this is that you should be careful not to reach a point where employees reach information overload but instead have a process in place that captures only the most useful information. Refreshing what is in your Knowledge Management System every six months becomes quite necessary as your overall system expands to contain more and more knowledge.

- Consolidations, acquisitions and globalization necessitate accessible knowledge. As roll-ups and consolidations continue to dot the services landscape, the ability of your services business to share information with newly acquired companies and across borders becomes paramount. Since mergers and acquisitions will certainly continue in the near future, s-businesses will not only be faced with the challenge of merging cultures successfully (a difficult task to say the least), but will also have the on-going challenge of creating the concept of a learning organization for everyone so that knowledge is not withheld or secretly stored away just in case it all does not work out.

Designing a Knowledge Management Structure

There are six steps to follow in structuring a framework for putting knowledge management into place:

1. Develop a knowledge strategy that is focused on everyone being able to access business "real-time" information anywhere and anytime.

2. Create an infrastructure that will enable the Knowledge Management System.

3. Design a culture change program that incorporates establishing a "learning organization."

4. Develop supportive work processes that enhance and improve the way professionals view how work is done.

5. Create the criteria by which knowledge will be selected and deselected over time.

6. Build a comprehensive communication program to introduce and incent individuals to use the Knowledge Management System.

Quite frequently services firms run initial contests to encourage everyone to log onto the new system. At the same time, holding everyone accountable for using the system is important as well. For example, a company had a section in its evaluation form that specifically addressed how frequently services professionals accessed the Knowledge Management System, as well as a section on specific performance targets related to how much each professional contributed to it monthly. Considering that knowledge is the key asset for most s-businesses, it makes a lot of sense to implement this particular best practice.

In the new reality of s-business, communicating successfully about your Knowledge Management System is critical. In this regard, a learning culture for your organization can be created through communication, education, and recognition. As shown in Table IX, a three-phase approach seems to work well.

All three phases are critical to your success. Communicating frequently through multiple channels creates awareness and understanding in order for the end users to gain a broader appreciation of how the systems should be used and leveraged. Training should involve demonstrating to end users how best to navigate through various processes but also provides hands-on application and involvement. It's also helpful to have a process in place to recognize the positive impact knowledge management can have on performance. Consequently, recognize those that have used the system for maximum benefit. Not

Table IX: The Three Phases of Communicating a KM System Successfully

Design a KM communications program	Build KM training for everyone	Reward and recognize KM successes
Announce program Create KM newsletter Create internal collaterals: programs, job aides	Incorporate KM into all training Provide KM orientations/ updates Structure multiple delivery channels: computer-based and coaching	Create tangible recognition programs that focus on utilization

only will your professionals appreciate the recognition but the process of recognition in and of itself will draw others to using the Knowledge Management System as well to gain the same benefit.

The Knowledge Management System needs to become a critical business issue. As one of the authors stated in an earlier work: "A professional services organization's knowledge base is its only true source of competitive advantage. So as professional services organizations add more and more people in more geographic areas and more services to meet client demands, the need for knowledge management (KM) transforms from a 'nice-to-do' functional objective to an organizational critical business issue" (Alexander, 1999, p. 11).

Furthermore, that same article identified the best ways to implement KM in any organization; based on the two main types of KM systems, *codification*, and *personalization* (Hansen, Nohria, and Tierney, 1999). Codification is a formal, document-driven approach that relies heavily on proprietary databases. The intent is that consultants can access all relevant data via modem with no (or minimal) one-to-one contact. Personalization, however, is driven by personal communications between people with knowledge and those wanting to acquire it. Databases are still used, but only as supplements to aid personal communications. The types of clients, products, services, and people your organization deals with will help you determine the correct focus for your organization. What we have seen is that many professional services firms successful in using KM have chosen to emphasize one or the other type, not both.

A few things to keep in mind as you move toward KM:

- *Effectively utilizing KM means that people must behave differently.* For KM to work, your best people (usually the busiest) will have to interrupt working on their projects and take considerable time sharing what they know with others in the organization. Role modeling behavior that you wish all employees to follow carries a lot of weight if your best people practice what they preach in utilizing the KM process themselves.

- *Keep KM simple at first.* Take a business unit that is most receptive to the idea to pilot your KM system. Learn from that prototype situation and let that success sell the rest of the organization on using KM.

- *There will be resistance, so involve lots of folks.* KM will affect everyone; their early input improves ideas and helps get buy-in to using the system. Get the feedback of high-profile clients and well-respected internal professionals. Keep those people you can't involve informed as the process moves along. Let people feel that they have the opportunity to participate in something that will impact in a good way on how they work.

Service Quality

One of the authors in an earlier publication (Alexander, 2001) pointed out that seminal work of three service marketing researchers (Parasuraman, Zeithaml, and Berry, 1985) showed the direct relationship between service quality and customer satisfaction, and identified five contributing dimensions:

1. *Reliability.* The ability to perform the promised service dependably and accurately

2. *Responsiveness.* The willingness to help clients and provide prompt service

3. *Assurance.* The knowledge and courtesy of employees and their ability to convey trust and confidence to clients

4. *Empathy.* The caring, individualized attention the firm provides its clients

5. *Tangibles.* The physical facilities of the services firm, its equipment, the technology it uses, and the appearance of its personnel

Further, the same article shared a very effective Service Quality Assessment tool that was adapted from the work of Parasuraman, Zeithaml and Berry (1985). That tool is illustrated in Figure 52 and should prove helpful to you in obtaining feedback on the service quality of your s-business.

The following are some tips that can be helpful when implementing the Service Quality Assessment:

- Do it over the phone. It greatly improves participation and takes ten minutes or less per survey.
- Offer clients a summary of your findings, comparing expectations scores against perceptions.
- Use the expectation-perception gaps to target performance improvement efforts.
- Communicate findings to your clients as well as to everyone in your organization.
- Institutionalize service quality by routinely tracking after each project and communicating overall scores on a regular basis.
- Make service quality an issue with your clients before engagements are sold. Put into the specs that service quality will be measured by both the client and the professional services organization.
- Get feedback during the project—don't wait until it's all over.
- Make service quality scores an element of both consultant evaluation and compensation.
- Promote your service quality prowess to differentiate your organization from the rest of the crowd.

Service Quality Assessment

Respondent: Date:

Please complete both sections of this short assessment (10 minutes or less) candidly. Your scores will be averaged with those of others and kept confidential.

Thank you for your feedback.

I. Your Expectations of Professional Service/S-Business Providers

This section deals with your expectations of the professional services providers you work with. Please pick a number that corresponds with how strongly you agree or disagree with each statement.

How much do you agree that services providers should...?

	Strongly disagree						Strongly agree
1. perform services right the first time.	1	2	3	4	5	6	7
2. complete actions by the time promised.	1	2	3	4	5	6	7
3. be dependable.	1	2	3	4	5	6	7
4. be reachable anytime, any way.	1	2	3	4	5	6	7
5. never be too busy to respond to a request.	1	2	3	4	5	6	7
6. explain exactly when and how you will be helped.	1	2	3	4	5	6	7
7. have up-to-date equipment and technology.	1	2	3	4	5	6	7
8. have visually appealing facilities.	1	2	3	4	5	6	7
9. have appropriate appearing personnel.	1	2	3	4	5	6	7
10. understand your specific issues and needs.	1	2	3	4	5	6	7
11. be consistently courteous.	1	2	3	4	5	6	7
12. instill confidence via their behaviors.	1	2	3	4	5	6	7
13. show a sincere interest in your problems.	1	2	3	4	5	6	7
14. give you individual attention.	1	2	3	4	5	6	7
15. have your best interest at heart.	1	2	3	4	5	6	7

II. Your Perceptions of ABC

How much do you agree that ABC...?

1. performs services right the first time.	1	2	3	4	5	6	7
2. completes actions by the time promised.	1	2	3	4	5	6	7

And so on...

Figure 52: Service Quality Assessment tool.

External Service Level Agreement

Creating and delivering on the service quality promise so that it meets expectations is one of the golden rules of s-business operations. At its highest level, it's a formal commitment to do as you say you are going to do (isn't that a unique idea). You will not only be judged on each project against this standard but it will serve as a criterion for selection in future work as well. Drilling down a bit further as you track service quality, you should also consider other types of measures that wrap a Service Level Agreement (SLA) within an external project. Although not intended to be an exhaustive treatise on what should get measured, Figure 53 highlights some tried and true categories that are often presented in external Service Level Agreements, particularly in outsourcing arrangements.

Internal SLAs

A discussion related to Service Level Agreements would not be complete without mentioning the importance of having an internal Service Level Agreement process as well. Simply stated, an internal Service Level Agreement process is a formal contract between the various functions in the services organization. It is built around the concept of shared ownership and service responsibility and accountability between functions of the organization.

The internal SLA can be a powerful s-business process to put into place for the following reasons:

1. It builds awareness inside the different areas of the services organization of various services that are offered by other functional areas of the company. (Many service areas of the company are totally unaware of what other groups do on a daily basis.)

2. It helps each functional area think through important issues such as: What services do we offer our internal partners? (It is unusual for any given functional area to have more than five or six key services they deliver to other areas of the organization.)

3. It helps internal functions come to terms with the "core" objectives they are trying to achieve.

1. Resources utilization. Most helpful when estimated, tracked, and reported back to the user department requesting the service.
2. Problem solution priority. Should be categorized by severity and importance codes, levels 1, 2, and 3.
3. Service requests for enhancements. You need to have a process to determine which enhancements get done first, second, etc.
4. Impact of priority on schedule or deadlines. Schedules can soon become outdated if not addressed as symptoms of problems start to appear.
5. Service availability. Needs to be classified by service types: ad hoc, problem management, enhancement, or project management.
6. Scores of user training. Always should be at least a 4.5 or higher on a 5.0 scale.
7. Time required to receive feedback based on requests. This also should have priority codes and be reported as a segment of time: one hour, one day, every week, etc.
8. Problem escalation process. Identification of who, what, when, and how others are notified in the event that a problem is critical. "Who gets the ball (the problem), who gets the call?"
9. User feedback. Without it, you will get lost quickly in what you think is important to the client's perspective. If in doubt, always ask the client.
10. Breaks in process flows, barriers identified and resolved. Processes can always be improved or enhanced. When everyone does not follow the standard processes, the client starts to experience a lack of consistency, and service quality will suffer.

Figure 53: Benchmarks of external SLAs.

4. It provides a framework for establishing measures for each area's internal services.
5. It provides an opportunity to examine how the services each area delivers could be improved from a pure process management perspective.

- A common organization-wide project/engagement tracking system is used.**
- Services management understands various leverage models.*
- A majority of product customers are under services contracts.*
- The cost of sales is tracked.*
- Key account profitability is tracked.*
  Customer/client loyalty is tracked.*

Figure 54: Operations best practices.

*   Statistically proven s-business differentiator from product-centered company.
**   Statistically proved practice of top-performing s-businesses.

6. It enables each functional service area to create a "balanced scorecard" for each service it delivers as well as a score for the entire services package.
7. It drastically improves communications and cross-functional teamwork, with a focus on meeting mutual expectations.

Caveat: Keep in mind that despite the benefits of the reports that PSAs and CRMs can provide, these software products can only automate that which you have in place. If you have a poor system and all the software does is to magnify it, it delivers no value. The end game is for you to change the processes and human performance that create the data in the first place.

Operations best practices are summarized in Figure 54.

Conclusion

At the end of the day, a balance needs to be struck between creating competitive advantage strategies for your s-business and striving to implement best practices on the operations side of the house. Like any enterprise, your ability to keep both of these in balance in critical for long-term success. Leverage enables you to make money and to expand. Knowledge management provides everyone with "intellectual capital" that enables your professionals to stay competitive. Service quality ensures reliable delivery and focusing on the right things before, during, and after each job engagement.

Chapter 8

S-Business Talent

RESEARCH FACTOID: In 86% of high-performing s-businesses, senior management is responsible for nurturing talent.

PONDER POINT: One great person can replace three good people.

PURPOSE: The purpose of this chapter is to explore talent best practices and the reality of developing star performers in your s-business organization. As service professionals, we are all keenly aware of the necessity of getting, growing, and keeping top performers. In the new s-business enterprise, the concept of developing stars who have the capability of producing three times the results of good performers (Harnish, 2002) is a goal worth pursuing. Figure 55 shows the enablers necessary for achieving that result. In this chapter we will explore various approaches to developing top talent, as well as how best to recruit, hire, develop, and retain "A" players. Issues related to the organization's culture, how to manage knowledge-workers, aligning the performance management system, and the requirements for developing talent when you choose a strategy that places your company in either a Vendor, Specialty, Total Solutions or Game Changer direction will also be addressed.

Identifying and Developing Star Performers

In every services company there are a group of star performers who are more productive, receive the highest customer satisfaction scores, and always exceed quota. These individuals overcome many organizational barriers and constraints that are often the result of poor planning, misalignment of resources, and sometimes a lack of organizational support. Star performers always stand out from the crowd as they possess unique knowledge and skills and have sharp instincts related to customer needs, wants, and issues.

The 3:1 performance ratio mentioned earlier is even more extreme in sales. As discussed in Chapter 5, when compared to average performers, stars in a services sales role can out-produce average performance by a factor of 7.

Star performers should be identified and selected based not on their potential but on the results they have actually delivered. Usually they are easy to find. They are the ones the customers always ask for, consistently receive the "top dog"

Figure 55: The talent success lever.

Talent

Recruiting
Hiring
Developing
Retaining

awards, and always volunteer to lead a task team even when they are twice as busy as everyone else. Simply ask around the company for who the star performers are and the list you generate will probably align with what the actual performance results show on the charts.

You can also determine how star performers do what they do by observing and interviewing them in different situations. For example you can ride along on sales and services calls, involve them in training workshops, and observe them running internal task teams to ascertain the behaviors they demonstrate as well as how they integrate and communicate their particular skills and abilities. Since most stars may not be aware of how they do what they do, running debriefing sessions and focus groups with them can yield many insights on the following topics:

1. How they overcome customer resistance
2. The key communications probes they use to gain the attention of customers
3. Through role-playing from both sides of the desk, what they and their customers are thinking and feeling at any given point in time in a selling situation
4. The four to six key things they always do when working with customers
5. Lessons learned and best practices
6. Critical incidents or "war stories" that provided them with the greatest learning experiences
7. How they lead with their strengths and how they minimize their deficiencies

All these characteristics can be captured and incorporated into job models and training design as well as used as benchmarks to compare against average performers. The gap that exists between these two groups then can serve as a benchmark from which new information can be applied so that the gap can be closed quickly. In addition, the output from this data gathering process can be built into a competence and capability profile for company-wide use.

Capabilities Assessment Profile

EXERCISE: Think about your personal client performance for the factors associated with each capability and circle your perception for each, then compute your total and average score.

	Strongly disagree	Strongly agree	Don't know
Relationship skills			
1. I am very good at building rapport.	1 2 3 4 5		☐
2. I am an efficient listener and prober.	1 2 3 4 5		☐
3. I effectively negotiate.	1 2 3 4 5		☐
4. I capably manage conflict.	1 2 3 4 5		☐
Business acumen			
5. I think and act like a business person.	1 2 3 4 5		☐
6. I am good at working at the "C" level.	1 2 3 4 5		☐
7. I understand critical business issues by level and function.	1 2 3 4 5		☐
Engagement management			
8. I create strong proposals.	1 2 3 4 5		☐
9. I am proficient at project management.	1 2 3 4 5		☐
10. I build appropriate metrics and accountability into my plans.	1 2 3 4 5		☐
11. I am good at solving problems throughout engagements.	1 2 3 4 5		☐
Technical expertise			
12. I am an expert in our technology.	1 2 3 4 5		☐

TOTAL SCORE = _____ AVERAGE SCORE = _____

Figure 56: Capabilities Assessment Profile.

Figure 56 contains the basic capability profile for the consulting capabilities introduced in Chapter 6. You can use it to determine the skills professionals possess today, and to ascertain those that need to be acquired in the future. When the entire organization has taken the profile, you can better calculate the future costs of hiring new people, training existing staff, or outsourcing your requirements. To determine which alternative is best for your organization, ask the following questions:

1. What is the impact of not closing the gaps that have been identified?
2. How large is the gap between the stars and average performers?
3. What type of training is most appropriate?
4. Where can talent be identified from other functional areas inside the company? (Quite often, for example, product sales professionals can become outstanding services sales stars if provided with the right training and given the right tools and support.)
5. How can we leverage our recruiting efforts, processes, and the external market to identify and recruit star performers? Where do they work and what would motivate them to come to work for our company?

Both identifying and developing star performers is a necessary requirement if your vision for the future is to become a high-performing s-business. Spending the time and effort to focus on these individuals can produce an enormous payback if you know the right questions to ask and can look in all the right places both inside and outside your services environment.

Managing Knowledge-Workers in an S-Business

Knowledge in an s-business can be the primary source of competitive advantage and at the same time the biggest barrier to entry into new markets. The emergence of knowledge management functions in most high-performing s-businesses also adds credence to the fact that knowledge is not only power but also the key asset for a successful services enterprise. However, capturing this knowledge is only part of the equation.

In most services organizations, the composition of the workforce will be made up of both technical services employees and knowledge-workers. Regardless of which particular organizational strategy you pursue—Vendor, Specialist, Total Solutions, or Game Changer—many of your professionals will be knowledge-workers. The knowledge they possess will have no real shelf life and will change rapidly as well as be widely dispersed through professional associations and networks. Their knowledge is also quite specialized, and their expertise has been finely tuned through specialized schooling and tenure with other similar services companies.

Managing knowledge-workers sounds sexy but it is at least one order of magnitude more challenging than managing either production or technical service workers, especially for those among us who are used to having "regular people" as direct reports (Alexander, 1999). As the new knowledge-worker manager quickly finds out, the consultants of the high-technology professional services industry are really a different breed. Some management techniques you may have used very successfully in the past, might very well work against you in this situation. Sure, the *concepts* of good management remain the same, but the *emphasis* is often quite different. There are three specific reasons for this:

1. *They know more than you do.* If these specialists don't know more than you in their areas of expertise, then you shouldn't have hired them in the first place. They don't need (or want) your advice. The implication here is that at best your unasked-for opinions will be politely tolerated before they are ignored. At worst your input will be seen as inappropriate, irksome meddling that will negatively impact both job performance and worker morale.

2. *They have different values.* Today's knowledge workers come hard-wired with a whole different idea about what work should look like and what they feel is important. They dislike bureaucracy, find politics distasteful, and despise incompetence. They require independence, expect the chance to learn and develop, and value working toward a worthy cause. Actually, it sounds to us like a pretty healthy way to look at the world.

3. *They vote with their feet.* As we all know, the demand for talented services providers far exceeds the supply (even in tough economic times), and the general high mobility of this workforce makes them susceptible to rapid employment changes.

They don't expect to receive loyalty from a corporation (or even a partnership) and therefore don't feel obligated to give it. They don't need your job and see no reason to tolerate what they consider inept management. Their allegiance is to their profession, not to their current employer.

So what is a manager of knowledge-workers to do? Switch positions? Retire? The answer requires a change in managerial mindset: *Treat knowledge workers as if they are volunteers.* Volunteers have no physical needs such as money or security to be met by an organization, only personal desires to be fulfilled by contributing to something they deem deserving.

Think about the situations in which you have volunteered your valuable time. Why did you do it? Before you made the commitment, we bet you asked yourself questions similar to these asked by most volunteers:

1. Does this outfit have its act together?
2. Is this a place where I can contribute?
3. Will I be challenged?
4. Will I be given responsibility *and* authority?
5. Can I grow here?
6. Will I be respected as the professional I am?
7. Is this a place with which I will be proud to be associated?

So we offer this as a checklist to grade and guide you on your knowledge-worker management effectiveness. Get some candid feedback on what the real responses are. If the answer to any of these seven questions is "no," then you have a problem that demands your immediate attention. Volunteers will only wait so long, then they will vote with their feet—and they often land in your competitor's camp ready and able to launch a frontal attack on your business.

One way to reduce the risk of losing your knowledge-workers and professional services staff is to regularly conduct a Top Talent Audit. Figure 57 shows the factors that make up a Top Talent Audit. Conducted at least yearly, this type of talent audit can quickly provide you with real-time information about

Top Talent Audit

	Strongly disagree ← → Strongly agree
Outside	
1. When accounts mention "the best and the brightest" your name comes up.	1 2 3 4 5 6 7 8 9 10
2. Your organization receives a constant flow of inquiries from candidates from top schools.	1 2 3 4 5 6 7 8 9 10
3. Your organization receives a constant flow of inquiries from experienced professionals from other firms.	1 2 3 4 5 6 7 8 9 10
4. Your services organization is quoted in the press as one of the best places to work.	1 2 3 4 5 6 7 8 9 10
Inside	
5. Every employee has a formal training program.	1 2 3 4 5 6 7 8 9 10
6. Every employee has a formal development program.	1 2 3 4 5 6 7 8 9 10
7. Retention of key employees is a critical management metric.	1 2 3 4 5 6 7 8 9 10
8. The compensation model is flexible when it comes to hiring top talent.	1 2 3 4 5 6 7 8 9 10
9. Rewards and recognition are provided to all who help in recruitment.	1 2 3 4 5 6 7 8 9 10
10. Top performers are encouraged to write and speak.	1 2 3 4 5 6 7 8 9 10
TOTAL SCORE = _____	

Figure 57: Top talent audit.

effective processes you have in place both outside and inside your services organization related to getting the best and the brightest. Concentrate on those areas of the audit where the gaps exist, and explore how these can best be closed as well as the impact they are having on the retention, motivation and creation of a strong pipeline of talent into your organization.

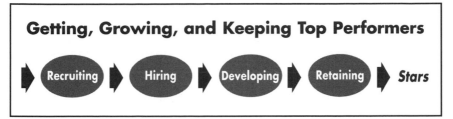

Figure 58: The star performer process.

The Star Performer Process

Inherent in any talent-building structure are four sub-processes that will need to be developed and enhanced over time based on best practices. As shown in Figure 58, these four areas are recruiting, hiring, developing, and retaining key people. To be successful in all four areas requires that each component be highly integrated and aligned to your overall business strategy, be it Vendor, Specialist, Total Solutions, or Game Changer.

Recruiting and Hiring Talent

Despite the fact that companies are hiring less for both economic and political market reasons, recruiting and retaining excellent employees is still very high on most companies' lists.

As stated by *Watson Wyatt's Human Capital Index® 2001/2002 Survey Report* (Watson Wyatt, 2001):

> When it comes to recruiting, which is undoubtedly still critical, the research shows that an investment of time more than pays for itself. Companies that step up their efforts to use formal strategies, align them with business plans, bring coworkers into the hiring process and then offer new hire orientations can be rewarded with 2.0 percent higher market value. (p. 8)

Clearly the role of recruiting in your s-business will not disappear. Consequently, understanding some current trends and "givens for the future" can aid you in leveraging your recruiting efforts to keep them in the forefront of effective change. Some important factors, trends, and practices to think about include the following:

1. Along with internal efforts, select a master partner to handle the bulk of the searches, and subcontract the rest.

2. Assign an executive in each business unit the responsibility of maintaining a database of prospective high-potential candidates.

3. Require candidate identification to be a part of every executive's responsibility and annual reviews.

4. Publish a quarterly newsletter communicating to all business units newsworthy items impacting recruiting and the delivery of talent.

5. Collect key recruiting metrics and align them with your services strategy.

6. Stay in contact with candidates throughout the entire recruiting process and if hired track their success in the company as their tenure grows.

7. Develop "fast-track" and "dual-track" recruiting and hiring processes. A fast-track process is utilized where you take a swat team approach for stellar services candidates such as a sales individual who has worked as a business development executive with a "Big 5" and also spent some time in the trenches of a startup software company. These candidates come with the experience of a big firm where all support needs have been provided as well as the experience of doing their own power point presentations in a startup environment where they wore multiple hats in the creation of a new company. The combination creates an individual with a high degree of resilience who will probably have quite a lot of flexibility to address new waves of change. A dual-track process also allows you to establish a career recruiting path that is not management-focused but services-technical-subject-matter-expert-focused. Some technical professionals prefer to never be a manager. Their interest is in becoming a subject matter expert instead.

8. Enhance your employee referral program. When people enjoy their jobs, they tell their friends. A great example of an

employee referral program that works can be illustrated by the approach taken by Stratus Computers. That organization parked a red mustang convertible across from the front entrance of the building to remind employees that the car could be theirs if they won a new-employee referral contest. Other services businesses simply use cash incentives if an employee referral stays for a designated period of time. Nobody will refer friends and colleagues to an organization that is a terrible place to work.

9. Tap into the "passive job market." Recruiters need to know how to investigate and identify top-performing, high-potential candidates who are not currently looking for new positions. Building research skills in how to find and leverage best practices, and how to utilize recruiting incentives, should be a part of every recruiter's training program.

Dashboard Talent Metrics You Should Track and Report

Measures of recruiting efficiency will continue to play a major role in the hiring tactics of s-business organizations. Figure 59 gives an example of the types of recruiting metrics you should consider using for your recruiting system.

Developing Talent

When was the last time you examined how you developed your services people? Can you articulate the causal relationship between how your top performers do their work and the results they achieve? Have you captured the prevailing best practices in developing professionals? Can you point to specific success cases and profile where a non-performer was successfully developed and became a top performer? All of these questions ideally drive home the point that development is a critical success factor in building successful s-business talent.

There are several primary ways to develop services talent: training, coaching, and using a performance management system that works. Together they form a strong foundation from which increased capabilities, skills, and competence can be sustained for the long term.

Financials	Performance
• Cost per hire • Open position aging • Retention rate	• Time to fill position • Acceptance rate • Cycle time (contact, interviews, offers, etc.
Internal Sourcing	**External Sourcing**
• Open position, percent inactive • Number of employee referral hires • Cost per employee referral	• Image, marketplace communications • Recruiter fees versus budget
Staffing	**Recruiters**
• Replacement rate • Time to start • Offer acceptance rate • Average sign-on bonus	• Average tenure • Productivity ratio/open requisition • Compensation rate • Human capital ROI
Communications	**Satisfaction**
• Effectiveness score of company materials • Number of quality contacts with candidates • Internal/external communications score • Good-will score	• Recruiter database/technology • Internal hiring manager • Candidate/pre-post hire • Partnership score with agencies/vendors

Figure 59: Recruiting metrics: balanced scorecard metric example.

TRAINING

The authors recently were retained to provide forty hours of consulting training for a large energy company that has as its goal to have over 1,000 of its internal consultants achieve the Certified Management Consultant designation from the Institute for Management Consulting (IMC), the only recognized global association offering this type of certification. Obviously this was a big commitment. Yet the energy company thought it was well worth the investment and effort. Pursuing certification for consultants and other knowledge-workers can greatly increase their credibility, building confidence in their abilities in the eyes of the buyers of your services.

In addition to certification programs, there are also two specific training best practices we have witnessed over the years that are worth mentioning:

1. *Training should be services-specific.* In a services environment, training should be services-specific. Since most service delivery will be focused on solving customer problems through some engagement management process, an in-depth understanding of service technologies, tools, and processes is a necessary fact of life. Training in relationship building and business development skills should also be part of your overall training plan, along with a certification process. As mentioned earlier in this chapter, your star performer analysis should serve as the key template upon which to build the training.

2. *Invest appropriately.* This is no area to be penny-wise and pound-foolish. How much of your gross revenue do you dedicate to training your professional staff? It is a best practice to invest heavily in training for your services staff. In this area, for example, Accenture sets the standard of excellence by allocating 6% of gross revenue to this purpose (data based on the experience of one of the authors while he was an executive with Andersen Consulting and as an instructor at its St. Charles global learning center from 1993-1998). Without a strong training effort, your consultants and IT professionals will quickly lose ground against the competition. Keep in mind it's what is "between the ears" that often will differentiate your employees from others in the marketplace. Keeping good people on board requires you to stay focused

on their on-going needs for tools training and tactics to deliver only high-impact and high-quality work to clients. Being multi-skilled is also important in that most services enterprises have quite a bit of overlap in their services. Knowing how it all fits together strategically and tactically often will give you an edge against competition.

COACHING

Coaching is an interactive process between a professional services employee and an immediate supervisor or mentor through which areas of skills and behavioral development are enhanced. A services coaching situation usually comes about as a result of the following situations:

- There is no *formal* business training or little or no skills training and the staff learns on-the-job, often working with a skilled practitioner. In this situation, coaching may take the form of feedback and evaluative reviews after completing a series of increasing engagement complexities.

- A *catch-up coaching* process focusing on specific areas of development is needed to bring the skills of staff members up to standards that may be new. This occurred in many professional services consulting firms when SAP subject matter experts had to be continually coached on new versions of the software and needed retraining on CRM when SAP began to cool in the marketplace as a sought-after skill for which demand was higher than the supply.

- *Opportunistic coaching* is required to meet a recognized need for retraining in newer concepts (for example, coaching staff members on how to make a successful transition from selling products to selling services).

- *Post coaching* may be needed as part of an institutionalized formal training process that has been established by the services organization. This may also include formal rotational programs tied directly to specific career development efforts that are in place. A good example of this situation is when directors need to provide coaching to consultants related to practicing business development techniques when they are on pure implementation assignments. In some professional services firms consultants may rotate through account representative and customer advocacy roles to provide them with the types of skills they will need with clients specific to relationship building. Despite having great technical skills, these professionals often lack customer relationship building skills to support the philosophy that everyone has a business development role in the company. Please note that coaching for other skill sets may also be needed to enhance employees' abilities to do their jobs well.

- A services staff member may need to spend time in IT systems integration, marketing, finance, and human resources in order to gain an understanding of the full life cycle of the business and its relationship to customers. In this situation, active *cross training* of internal resources across multiple business disciplines requires multi-levels of feedback from those who have worked with the services staff member.

- An employee is not meeting expectations, resulting in a performance gap, and you need to have that person coached on better working habits to close the gap. Or perhaps you want employees coached to reinforce certain behaviors.

In all these situations, your ability to be an effective coach will depend upon your own ability to handle the coaching situation in a manner that will produce the desired result (reinforcement, enhancement, or improvement) in performance. Listed below are some guidelines to follow that will help you achieve the type of coaching results you desire. All are important when your goal is to create the right supportive environment for communications to foster learning and skills enhancement.

1. Identify and capitalize on the employee's strengths.
2. Establish standards of excellence.
3. Agree upon what the priorities are and should be.
4. Solicit ideas as to what each of you would like to get out of the coaching session.

5. Jointly discuss the pros and cons of each new idea presented.
6. Provide feedback where the staff member has done well and find ways to transfer those identified areas of success to new areas of need.
7. Identify formal training that can be supportive of on-going coaching.
8. Provide the staff member with supportive information to review and read related to services trends, best practices, and knowledge. Assign some homework related to this information for the next several coaching sessions.
9. Summarize key points that you have covered in the coaching session.
10. Encourage the employee to generate alternative ideas.
11. Demonstrate confidence that the employee has the ability to solve problems. In this regard, part of the dialogue needs to focus on your sharing the company's larger strategic or business picture in order to help the employee see how his or her work fits into the greater scheme of things.
12. Schedule a follow-up meeting to review progress.

THE PERFORMANCE MANAGEMENT SYSTEM

We have worked with many services organizations that have done exceptional jobs of providing talented people with training and interesting engagements, and that have developed excellent engagement methodologies to follow. However, despite all these positive elements, when you look under the covers of those organizations, what you often find is a fragmented, ineffective performance management system in place that acts in direct opposition to what the company would like to accomplish! For example, if you tell your sales people that you expect them to sell services yet only reward them for selling boxes, guess what they will do?

Recently, in assisting a software company that derives 40% of its revenues from its services division, the client shared with us a very polished engagement management process that the company's consulting groups had available to them through its knowledge management program. When we asked if the consultants followed this process, we were told 50% did and the rest did not. When we further investigated the reasons the consultants refused to utilize the engagement process, we were told that there were no consequences for not using the methodology. In addition, other elements that would have supported its use were also missing: There was no reference to its use in everyone's performance evaluations, there was poor support from the technology groups, and there was a general lack of feedback and reviews on its use.

Figure 60 shows the five factors making up a performance system that is applicable to any job (Alexander, 1999b). All the factors must align and support each other if maximum performance is to have a chance of being obtained.

Figure 61 shows a performance checklist system for a consultant's business development responsibilities. Take a few minutes and complete it for your organization. Ideally for each component of this system your individual and collective responses should fall within the "strongly agree" category as it relates to actual practices that are in place. For any of your responses that

Figure 60: The performance system.
Source: Adapted from Alexander, 1999b.

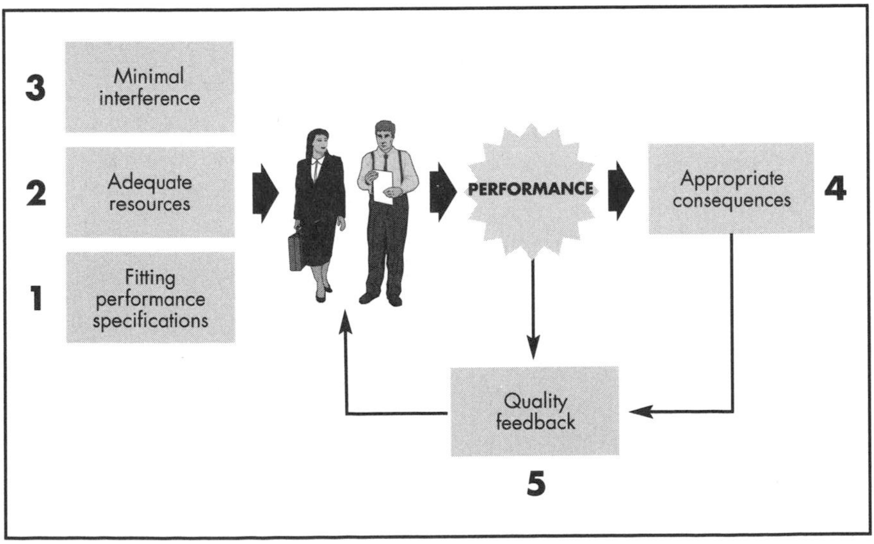

Performance System Checklist:
Business Development Example
Performer=Consultant

	Strongly disagree	Strongly agree	Don't know
1. Fitting performance specifications			
A. Clear performance specifications exist.	1 2 3 4 5		☐
B. Performance specifications are realistic.	1 2 3 4 5		☐
C. Performance specifications align with each other.	1 2 3 4 5		☐
D. Performance specifications support the business strategy.	1 2 3 4 5		☐
2. Adequate resources			
A. Performers have the information they need when they need it.	1 2 3 4 5		☐
B. Performers have necessary staff support.	1 2 3 4 5		☐
C. Performers have enough time to do the job.	1 2 3 4 5		☐
D. Performers have the appropriate tools.	1 2 3 4 5		☐
3. Minimal interference			
A. Job procedures are logical.	1 2 3 4 5		☐
B. Non-value-adding tasks are seldom imposed on performers.	1 2 3 4 5		☐
4. Appropriate consequences			
A. Consequences are aligned to support desired performance.	1 2 3 4 5		☐
B. Consequences are meaningful to performers.	1 2 3 4 5		☐
C. Consequences are timely.	1 2 3 4 5		☐
5. Quality feedback			
A. Feedback is relevant.	1 2 3 4 5		☐
B. Feedback is accurate.	1 2 3 4 5		☐
C. Feedback is timely.	1 2 3 4 5		☐
D. Feedback is specific.	1 2 3 4 5		☐
E. Feedback is easy to understand.	1 2 3 4 5		☐

TOTAL SCORE = _____   OVERALL AVERAGE = _____

Figure 61: Performance System Checklist: business development example.

are in the "strongly disagree" category, further investigation and tracking of the impact of not addressing these areas need to occur. Paying attention to the five areas will lead to a higher level of performance from your services professionals. One area in particular (Appropriate consequences) will make a significant difference if the consequences are aligned to support the desired performance and are meaningful to your services professionals. Think of how customer satisfaction could be increased by the software company we described that only had a 50% compliance rate on using its engagement management process if the other 50% of its consultants also followed the engagement management process as it was intended to be utilized. The following could occur:

- Greater leverage of prior work could be captured.
- Quality feedback in each step of the process would be identified before problems escalated.
- Clients would receive a higher degree of consistency in the work on their projects as hand offs occurred between the various consultants who came onto the projects.
- Identified new opportunities would not be missed as leads could be effectively entered into the CRM process.
- Performance delivery could be tracked and measured successfully.
- Integration from various projects could be communicated and coordinated effectively.

All of the areas identified in the performance system are important and need to be part of your overall approach to strengthening the talent process in your organization.

TROUBLESHOOTING PERFORMANCE PROBLEMS

Figure 62 is a simple diagnostic useful for determining problems in existing performance and identifying clues as to the root causes. Let's use the same example from above, the consultant's role in business development. If the vast majority of the consulting organization falls into the "willing and able" quadrant, all is well. Just keep doing what you are doing. If your answer is

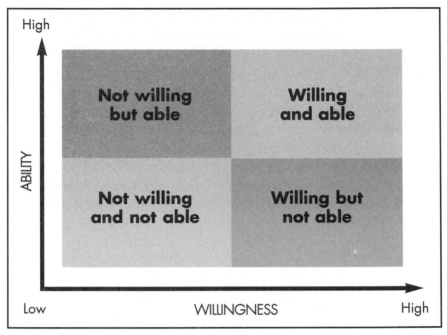

Figure 62: Role and performance matrix.

"not willing but able," your people have the requisite knowledge and skills, so they don't need training. The problem is a motivational one and the solution lies in changing the performance management system to encourage business development behavior and discourage non-action. If you feel that the majority of the consulting organization falls into the "willing and not able" box, then yup, training and coaching is called for. Finally, if you end up in the "not willing and not able" quadrant, all aspects must be addressed. First adjust the performance system to get people to want to develop business, next deliver quality services-specific, business development training, and then reinforce it all with one-on-one coaching.

Retaining Talent

In "Human Performance: Stemming the Tide" by Tony Clancy and Armaud Andre (published in the January 2001 issue of Accenture's online *Outlook Journal*), the authors clearly lay out what is needed to retain talent in today's marketplace:

Companies everywhere are struggling to hold on to their most important valuable employees. But the war for talent can be won—with new programs that combine competitive compensation with better communications, a wide range of personal growth opportunities and a clearer articulation of standards and expectations.

And according to reports from the California-based Saratoga Institute, attrition rates at U.S. companies have increased by nearly 20 percent during the past five years, to an average rate of 16.5 percent. At European companies, employee turnover was up 10 percent in 1999 to an average of 14 percent, according to Saratoga Europe. Making a bad situation worse is the fact that the attrition rate for new hires is nearly 30 percent in the first year of employment.

So what is the best way to retain staff? In the list below, we highlight a few of the best practices and effective strategies that have helped services companies stay ahead of the curve and keep attrition rates within respectable ranges:

- Rotating professionals among functional areas and divisions as well as having them work on a series of diverse limited-term assignments to keep them motivated and engaged
- Organizing talent exchanges between offices, countries, and divisions that enable staff members to experience different aspects of the company's culture and local processes
- Setting up mentoring programs organized by race, experience, and gender, and even for wives/husbands of employees
- Providing access to computer-based case-based simulations
- Linking compensation to competitive benchmarks as well as to performance system use
- Developing clear performance expectations and making them known to employees
- Creating talent networks with alliance partners, third-party vendors, and part-timers to enable staff to get exposure to outside knowledge and skills that are often transferable to their jobs inside the company

- Making a knowledge management system that is user-friendly and supports a learning organization accessible to employees
- Providing positive feedback when an employee does a good job (no reputations as the "Boss from Hell" allowed!)
- Seeing that human relations and communications skills are highly valued throughout every part of the organization and practiced every day
- Communicating support for career/family values
- Fostering high-quality and focused supervision and leadership
- Awarding additional compensation to employees who achieve certified management consultant (CMC) status, receive certification from the Project Management Institute (PMI), receive CPA or MBA degrees, and the like
- Providing stock options and other total company incentives
- Providing pay premiums for hard-to-find and deep skills

Successful retention in an s-business organization also requires you to have a positive mindset specific to what's in it for your employees, your organization, and you, the s-business executive. These are important questions in that they not only create a positive dialogue but also ideally bring everyone together on the same page working toward the goal of strong retention.

Here are some things to ponder as you consider your own responses to these questions:

1. *What's in it for your employees?* When retention is high, people feel more secure and have less concern related to the performance of the company in weathering the storms that often plague organizations. They also build relationships and networks for support, knowledge sharing, and teamwork.

2. *What's in it for your organization?* Being known as a best place to work not only helps the recruiting process but positions your company where you want it to be in the eyes of your potential customers and clients. It tells them you have sustainability and experience based on a group of employees who have the skills and abilities needed to do the work. It

also helps your costs to stay in line, as we all know it is much more costly to bring a new employee up the learning curve than it is to utilize existing staff that are already producing.

Although somewhat controversial, we note that we also feel an s-business probably needs to be trimming its ranks at least 10% a year to enable new high performers to come into the company. Under current economic and market conditions, you cannot afford to keep non-performers very long. Let's not forget that the goals of every business are to earn a profit, to generate revenue, and to grow. Sometimes you just don't have the right people to make that happen.

Linking Talent Requirements to the Four S-Business Strategies

In previous chapters we have discussed the four strategies (Vendor, Specialist, Total Solutions, and Game Changer) a services organization should consider. Each of these particular strategies has a specific impact on the type of talents needed.

Vendors

With a Vendor strategy, the organization is typically run as a Lean and Mean enterprise focused on low costs. In this regard, the type of individuals it typically recruits and develops are people who can be trained to deliver a consistent quality of service specifically tailored to the services provided to the company clients. As an example, services companies that provide training to support software will utilize a variety of professionals to deliver that training: contractors, adjunctive consultants, and other alliance partners. Some even outsource the function to another organization that can manage the entire process. The ultimate goal is to provide a common face to the client based on either some certification process or pre-packaged materials that provide the trainers with scripts to follow. The depth of experience of the services providers is limited to the particular services offering and the performance expectation is aligned to a very specific deliverable provided in a very specific way so that costs and overhead are kept in line.

Specialists

A Specialist strategy provides world-class capabilities in very selected areas. This strategy typically positions the services staff as experts in particular areas: SAP, CRM, ERP, supply chain management, managed services, or a particular industry such as energy, government, etc. Consequently the approach of such organizations to talent is very specific, as they seek out services professionals that have both subject matter expertise and deep experience in all phases of the particular functional area the company services. Such professionals often lack the flexibility to expand their expertise to other parts of the company as most of their time and energy is dedicated to gaining as much experience as possible in their areas of focus. When you engage these professionals, you get people with deep knowledge and access to often proprietary knowledge and methodologies.

Professional services consulting firms like Jefferson Wells International, which focuses on the financial services industry, will only hire people that have a minimum of ten years of experience in finance. They will not recruit off-campus, and their market message to a prospective client is that the experience of their staff members in the client's market and business is a very compelling reason to engage them.

Total Solutions

The Total Solutions strategy, on the other hand, seeks staff members that have the potential to work in multiple areas of a company. Their services professionals are quite adept at multi-tasking and often come to the client with broad experience in multiple industries. Their professionals have strong selling skills as well as engagement management expertise. PriceWaterhouseCoopers is a good example of a consulting firm that has positioned its professionals as individuals who can provide Total Solutions in terms of strategy, change management, process, and the technology aspects of the client's business.

Total Solutions firms not only recruit heavily on-campus, but also seek out experienced hires that often serve as mentors to junior-level staff. They also invest heavily in training in organizational methodologies and best practices. Talent in these organizations is profiled as having a strong breadth of capabilities that can provide one-stop shopping in meeting client needs. In this regard, the staff members of Total Solutions organizations often have greater career development opportunities as they can focus on multiple areas of service provision and redirect their career paths to areas of their greatest strength. Professionals in these services companies usually work well in teams as they bring to the table a broad understanding of services, business, and the impact of service actions on all parts of the client's company.

Game Changers

Game Changer organizations operate at the highest levels of "thought-leadership" when it comes to innovation and breakthrough. Professionals in these organizations are primarily recruited from the top business schools and bring to the table a knowledge base that focuses on how to analyze a services enterprise from a strategic perspective. They are constantly being asked by clients to find out how to reach the next orbit of success or where the next breakthrough will be as to markets, customers, or services. Skill building in Game Changer services companies follows a very tight career path and is structured to leverage multiple ways to see the world of services.

The ultimate professional in these services firms believes in the concept of "breakthrough" and focuses on those critical few overlooked concepts or possibilities that will produce the greatest return for company efforts. Additionally, Game Changer organizations invest heavily in market intelligence and research and expect their professional staff to participate actively in market research projects. The findings from these types of efforts are coupled with marketing initiatives through the publication of books and participation in industry conferences, which staff members are expected to attend.

Talent Best Practices

Building new capabilities for your s-business will require that you put into place a variety of best practices in order for your company to be well positioned and to fully leverage the skills and capabilities of your professionals

Here are the ten best and core practices identified in the s-business research (Alexander, 2002) (for a summary see Figure 63):

1. *Recruiting is viewed as a key business process.* When viewed as a key business process, recruiting is given the attention it needs to obtain the funding and investments it requires to attract only the best potential hires to an organization. With competition at your door every day, you can ill afford to have top talent work for your competitors. Seeing recruiting as a key business process helps sharpen the lens inside the company to enable this process to work effectively and efficiently.

2. *The realities of the experienced hire marketplace are understood.* Most organizations sort through thousands of resumes they

Figure 63: Talent best practices.

*   Statistically proven s-business differentiator from product-centered company.

1. Recruiting is viewed as a key business process.
2. The realities of the experienced hire marketplace are understood.
3. Compensation is regularly benchmarked.
4. The best talent is hired regardless of immediate need.
5. Mentoring programs are in place.
6. A recruiting system is in place.*
7. A talent development system is in place.*
8. Capability profiles are in place for each position in the services organization.*
9. Senior management is responsible for nurturing talent.*
10. "Alumni networks" are in place to maintain relationships with past employees.*

receive every day. Few service organizations truly understand how to research, target, and "romance" star performers who are working for other companies and have no immediate interest in leaving their current employers. Training your recruiters in how to conduct research into the "passive" market along with developing skills in how to motivate potential hires to change companies is an activity worth investing in.

3. *Compensation is regularly benchmarked.* For many services companies, the ability to retain key performers is contingent upon their ability to stay abreast of compensation trends in their industry. Conducting compensation studies at least twice a year to ensure you are not falling behind in how star performers are paid enables you to be at least in parity with your competitors and is not an immediate de-selector from the candidate's perspective. You may not always be able to match or beat what the market is paying, but at least you will know how to address that issue with other benefits and incentives when the objection is raised in the hiring process.

4. *The best talent is hired regardless of immediate need.* When you spot an individual who can make the world move in his or her direction, hire them regardless of immediate need. That kind of talent is rarely in over-supply and their work inside and outside your company not only will be contagious but also can be leveraged to create new opportunities.

5. *Mentoring programs are in place.* Everyone needs a mentor from time to time. This is especially true for the services enterprise, where skills and experience levels may vary greatly and your primary interest is to retain talent for the long term. Mentoring programs can play a vital role in helping new professionals assimilate quickly to your culture and understand the realities of how best to move ahead in the organization. They also act as a support process during situations where employees find themselves between a rock and a hard place. A safe harbor to discuss options and different ways to see things can often turn the tide for an employee who only sees frustration and difficulty in maximizing their potential for the company.

6. *A recruiting system is in place.* Recruiting is never a one-shot event, and with so many different channels available to you today—Web-based screening tools, behavioral screens, alumni networks, various types of search firms, etc.—a complete and comprehensive system needs to be developed to ensure you are tapping into the right talent pools inside and external to the company.

7. *A talent development system is in place.* Service companies are dependent upon having the right skills available to match various services needs. In order to build that capability and those skills for all your staff, a well-defined system to provide on-going training, rotation programs, etc., needs to be a part of every individual's capability building process.

8. *Capability profiles are in place for each position in the services organization.* A capability profile outlines where your services staff members have strengths and where they require developmental improvement. Every position should have one.

9. *Senior management is responsible for nurturing talent.* In s-business organizations, senior management plays a vital role in identifying key talent and is also responsible and accountable for a sustainable pipeline of future star players. Both evaluative factors and incentives to identify talent and to support them through the recruiting process demonstrates to the entire organization the importance of the recruiting process, and also fast-tracks key players from identification through commitment.

10. *"Alumni networks" are in place to maintain relationships with past employees.* People leave organizations for many reasons. Some have had great experiences with a firm but find it's time to move on to greater heights. In the case where the experience has been positive, developing alumni Web pages and networks can be an effective link for future referrals as well as for motivating key previous employees to rejoin the company. Accenture (formerly known as Andersen Consulting), as an example, does a very effective job at keeping in contact with its previous employees. On its alumni network

page you can read thought-leadership articles, join a particular community, find lost colleagues, as well as explore new opportunities. The site is quite user-friendly as well as focused on keeping you abreast of what the firm is doing, where it is headed, and what other alumni are up to. All and all, developing this type of alumni recruiting structure is a good idea and one to be followed by forward-thinking organizations.

Conclusion

Someone once said, "Everyone has talent. What is rare is the courage to follow that talent into uncharted territory." The s-business enterprise along with its dedicated professionals must have the courage to be a best-practices organization but also continue to motivate its professional staff to always reach for the highest level of performance so there are only "A" players in the organization.

PART THREE

Leaping the Chasm

This section is for any reader looking at improving performance, but is especially valuable to those on the left side of the chasm—Position 3 on the S-Business Continuum—who have decided to help lead/cajole, prompt, urge, beg, his/her organization to change its orientation because the benefits of transitioning to s-business far outweigh the potential risks of standing still.

Chapter 9 will explore the critical importance of culture, the three core elements of adaptive culture, and how to change the culture if required. Chapter 10 will outline the three-phase process for transitioning from "today's business-as-usual" to tomorrow's "business-as-exceptional"—becoming a top-performing s-business.

The reader should note that this section is designed to be an actionable workbook—tools are presented and the serious agent of change is invited to do his/her own analysis and plan as he/she works through Chapters 9 and 10.

Chapter 9

Creating a High-Performance S-Business Culture

RESEARCH FACTOID: Organizations with healthy cultures increased net income 756% over an 11-year period compared to a 1% increase for everybody else.

PONDER POINT: Culture is to the organization what personality is to the individual.

PURPOSE: This chapter will help you create and sustain a high-performance culture by:
- Understanding the dramatic performance potential of an adaptive s-business culture
- Considering the "dark side"—the negative ramifications of a strong culture gone bad
- Aligning your culture to your specific services strategy
- Learning the three core elements of any great culture
- Finding out how to assess your current culture and the steps required to make positive changes

As the leaders of services organizations reexamine, rethink, and sometimes reinvent their business models in light of an uncertain economy and a continually shifting marketplace, all components of their paradigm should be scrutinized for appropriateness, fit, and improvement potential. A key contributor (although often overlooked) to organization performance is its culture. The greater the degree of change required, the more befitting it is to re-look at the existing culture to predict whether it will be a catalyst in moving the organization ahead or act as an impediment, staunchly defending the status quo.

There is a strong justification for considering organization culture as a primary lever of performance and a driver of reinvention. Figure 64 presents the key findings from a study comparing the financial success of high-performance, adaptive cultures versus the non-high performing non-adaptive corporate cultures (Kotter and Heskett, 1992). The results are dramatic. The non-high performers' increased net income just 1% over an eleven-year period compared to 756% improvement for the organizations identified as having high-performance cultures. Major differences appeared as well when comparing the other factors of revenue growth, workforce expansion, and stock-price growth. This performance potential of organization culture cannot be ignored.

So What Do You Mean By Culture Anyway?

Here are some definitions of culture to think about:

A pattern of shared, basic assumptions that the group learned as it solved its problems of external adaptation and internal integration, that has worked well enough to be considered valid and, therefore, to be taught to new members as the correct way to perceive, think and feel in relation to those problems. (Schein, 1992, p. 12)

The basic fabric and beliefs of the organization's "way of life" based on assumptions that have been espoused or that have evolved over time. This includes:

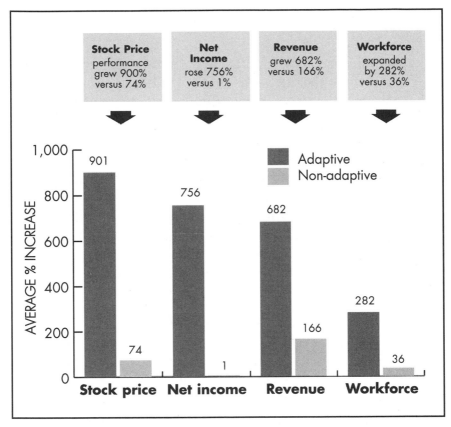

Figure 64: Culture impact on long-term economic performance (eleven-year time frame).

- Individual and company norms, values, and beliefs
- Extent to which "politics" are important
- Management/supervisory style or philosophy
- Attitudes toward employees
- Measures of success (Andersen Consulting, n.d.)

Culture governs the way a company processes information, its internal relations, and its values. It functions at all levels from subconscious to visible. It defines appropriate behavior, bonds and motivates individuals and asserts solutions where there is ambiguity. (Hampton–Turner, 1992, p. 13)

The way we do things around here. (Burke and Litwin, 1989, p. 7)

What is apparent from all these definitions are some fundamental concepts that relate to shared beliefs, assumptions, and behaviors that are acquired over time by members of an organization. Ideally these attributes become habitual over the years and, as a result, people begin to think, feel, and act in a manner that supports a business perspective, strategy, or direction. No matter how you define culture in your services organization, it should have a lot to do with what's really important and link directly to supporting your services strategy. Without this specific connection to strategy, one could argue that culture is just about feel-good words and not the good business sense that models values, generates motivation, and drives performance.

Characteristics of Organization Culture

Organization culture is created when the early leaders of the organization, usually the founders, make decisions and take action (by skill, dumb luck, or a combination of the two) based on their personal views of the world. If these actions work, the leaders continue to apply their specific models of thinking, decision making, and actions to other issues, and if success continues, a culture embodying these predictable patterns is gradually formed over time.

As the culture matures, members of the organization begin to implicitly share a set of common values and to explicitly share a set of accepted behaviors. If the organization proves to be very successful, then stories, and sometimes myths, form around the founder or founders. Recounting these heroic tales further inculcates the organization with powerful examples of success achieved by thinking and acting in the "correct way." So the culture of the organization defines the norms (and thus the acceptable boundaries) of individual and team behavior. Over time, as long as success continues, the culture becomes highly ingrained to the point of becoming invisible to the members of the organization. That is why it is so difficult for group members to talk about their culture, because it operates at a level below normal consciousness.

Of course, all organizations have subcultures, such as functions where the credos and behaviors, say, of members of the consulting group might be (and almost always are) different from those of people who work in accounting. Furthermore, location has an impact on culture. A Latin American group probably will have elements of its culture quite different from those of an Asian Pacific group. However, an organization with a strong culture will share certain elements across all aspects of the organization. This can be a very helpful factor. It serves as an organizational shorthand, and many actions and reactions can be implemented swiftly, as there is no need for debate because everyone who has been around for a while "knows" the correct things to do (or at least the range of acceptable alternatives). On the other hand, culture abhors change and will dramatically resist any idea that falls outside its framework of acceptable behavior. By its nature, it tries to preserve the tried and true. This makes perfect sense in an organization with a history of achievement. Why rock the boat when there is already a proven approach to success?

As long as the culture aligns with and supports an appropriate strategy, the stronger the culture, the more effective the organization. In this scenario, it is the services leader's role to reinforce the existing culture by modeling, encouraging, and rewarding "sanctioned" behavior. As Edgar Schein (1992, p. 1) puts it, "Leadership and culture are two sides of the same coin. Leaders create and change cultures, while managers live within them."

Aligning the Culture to the Services Strategy

So that means services leaders need a tool to help them understand the important cultural factors and how they relate to services strategy. Table X shows five dimensions that shape organization culture, along with a scaled range of behaviors for each

Table X: Culture Dimensions

Dimension	1 2 3 4 5 6 7 8 9 10	
View of time	Past	Future
Pace	Slow	Fast
Group orientation	Team	Individual
Power	Procedures	People
Value	Process	Ideas

one. Our purpose is not to label any point on the scale as good or bad, merely to contrast the differences. However, it should be pointed out that some behaviors are more appropriate for certain strategies than others. Also, understanding these dimensions will be important later as we talk about both aligning services culture with product culture and blending services cultures during mergers or acquisitions. Those dimensions are as follows:

- *View of time:* This dimension helps determine whether the organization's main tendency is past-oriented or future-oriented. For example, a view of time that looks more toward the past is appropriate for Vendors since they need to scrutinize the past actions of other services organizations that are successful and adapt those practices to their organization. Yet this same past-oriented view of time would be very inappropriate to a Game Changer, as its innovation orientation must be squarely focused on the future to be successful. Total Solutions Providers for the most part should be focused on the present also as they attempt to take the hottest issues and deal with them. Specialists should be between Total Solutions Providers and Game Changers. Misalignment in this dimension (or any of the others) causes stress in the culture.
- *Pace:* Since speed is a strategic tool, most organizations should be more "fast" than "slow."
- *Group orientation:* The power of well-oiled teams has been proven, and a strong team orientation, for example, is a necessity in implementing a Total Solutions strategy well. However, the new concepts and ideas required of Game Changers and

Specialists often are generated by individuals, and hence too strong a team orientation can be detrimental. Both of these strategies need to have an individual orientation.

- *Power:* The business books are full of talk of empowerment and the need for individuals to take charge of the situations they face. A perfect example is the importance of services providers at "the moment of truth" taking the initiative to meet changing and challenging customer issues. We strongly believe in this concept. However, the degree of "power disbursement" should vary depending on what the services organization is trying to accomplish. For example, for Vendors to be successful, they need strong, streamlined processes and procedures. We have pointed out that this is critical to their success. Hence, power for them is embedded in following "rules"—following a well-established set of steps. However, at the other extreme Game Changers are trying not only to change the rules but to change the game. Here the power of the s-business must be in its key people, which means a much much looser, flexible, adaptive organization is required.

- *Value:* Vendors value process since it is the key to efficiency. Total Solutions Providers also lean toward the process side, as their ability to control projects and engagements are key determinants of profitability. Game Changers and Specialists respect the importance of process but really value the power of ideas since ideas are the engine of innovation.

Many other dimensions can be used to classify cultural differences, but hopefully this section made the point that certain cultural dimensions align better with certain strategies.

The Dark Side of Organization Culture

There is a darker side to organization culture, as it can blind people to facts that don't match its assumptions, and even the smart, experienced, and successful executives of services organizations can fall prey to this problem. The culture acts as a filter that sifts out information that doesn't fit the organization's view of the world. Or if information does make it through the screen, it is either distorted to fit within the existing framework of reality or it is heartily denied as being insignificant, flat wrong, or just plain crazy. Obviously, this cultural sieve can be a significant detriment in a business world traveling at e-speed, where completeness and accuracy of data are contributors to competitive advantage. Common sense, rational thought, and experience are no longer virtues when they are based on a flawed reality.

There are three warning signs for cultures out of control (Kotter and Heskett, 1992):

1. Managers appear arrogant.
2. While often decreeing just the opposite, managers in unhealthy cultures tend not to highly value all constituencies.
3. Managers actively resist acts of "leadership" and often are hostile toward any attempts of significant change. In these organizations, the underlying culprit of this resulting elitism has almost always been long-term success and a lack of strong competition. In such cases, leadership has not been needed, and a strong managerial orientation has taken place—one that places a high value on stability and order. These are the organizations most susceptible to nimble, outside challengers because they never see (or acknowledge) the new competition until it is too late.

The Three Core Elements of Healthy Cultures

Earlier, we described the benefits of a strong culture, but those benefits remain benefits only as long as a culture is supportive of the organization's strategy and appropriate for today's marketplace. We also know that the stronger the culture, the more resilient it is to change, and services firms are no different from other organizations in this respect (Maister, 1997). So the very things that made the organization strong and prosperous in the past may be the exact elements that block success tomorrow. The more successful an organization is, the more its culture will resist any and all changes. So what can one do to sustain perfor-

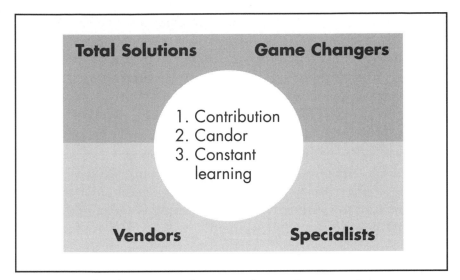

Figure 65: The three core elements of an adaptive culture.

mance? The challenge, and the paradox, lie in conceptualizing and creating a culture in which perpetual change is one of the stable elements (Schein, 1992). Accomplishing this allows the culture to maintain its strength while constantly adapting to shifts in the environment. There are three core elements of cultures that are both adaptable across culture models and sustainable over time (Figure 65) (Alexander, 1999). The three components are contribution, candor, and constant learning. Together, they embrace change and allow each culture model to excel in its unique area of strength.

Contribution refers to the actual value added by either the individual or the group or groups within which people operate. Contribution is a part of a culture when (1) results are valued more than hard work, (2) performance is more important than political connections in getting recognized and rewarded, (3) individuals are expected to take personal responsibility for their actions, and (4) there is a tolerance of unusual styles in the behavior of the people who do good work. *Candor* has been identified as a critical requirement for overcoming an organization's defensive barriers (Argyris and Schön, 1996). Candor is a part of a culture when (1) people are frank, even when the ideas of employees directly contradict those of superiors, (2) people challenge the unsupported talk and actions of others, (3) people routinely stop to reflect about what they are doing and why, and (4) exemplary performers are regularly observed and analyzed to fuel improvement efforts. *Constant learning* has special significance in making a culture amenable to change, because in order to constantly learn, an organization must actively listen, understand, and align with the issues and the feelings of all its stakeholders. Organizations with this element built-in are open to ongoing change because they see meeting stakeholder needs as an element of the culture. Constant learning is a part of a culture when (1) continuous improvement is valued, (2) innovation is prized, (3) appropriate knowledge-management systems are in place, and (4) quality failure is acceptable.

To gain a sense of where your organization is today in terms of the three core elements of an adaptive culture (Alexander, 2001), take the assessment shown in Figure 66 to best calibrate which of the elements are your strengths and which need your attention for future action.

Special Challenges of Blending Cultures

Shortly we will outline the steps to effectively bringing about culture change. However, a couple considerations need to be mentioned first.

Product-Services Cultural Conflict

As we've tried to point out, product people think and act differently than services people, and this is reflected in their cultures. Since these cultural "world views" are so different, for many members of product-centered companies the thought of changing their business strategy and making the cultural shift to a services-driven business can be quite scary. Resistance is natural and must be anticipated. Employees must be provided with an understanding of the cultural similarities and the critical differences between product-centered and services-centered organizations before the change in the culture is begun.

Adaptive Culture Audit

	Strongly disagree		Strongly agree

Contribution

1. Results are valued more than hard work. 1 2 3 4 5 6 7 8 9 10

2. Performance is more important than political connections in getting recognized and rewarded. 1 2 3 4 5 6 7 8 9 10

3. Individuals are expected to take personal responsibility for their actions. 1 2 3 4 5 6 7 8 9 10

4. There is a tolerance of unusual styles of behavior of the people who do good work. 1 2 3 4 5 6 7 8 9 10

Candor

5. People are frank, even when ideas directly contradict those of superiors. 1 2 3 4 5 6 7 8 9 10

6. People challenge the unsupported talk and actions of others. 1 2 3 4 5 6 7 8 9 10

7. People routinely stop to reflect about what they are doing and why. 1 2 3 4 5 6 7 8 9 10

8. Exemplary performers are regularly observed and analyzed to fuel improvements. 1 2 3 4 5 6 7 8 9 10

Constant learning

9. Continuous learning is valued. 1 2 3 4 5 6 7 8 9 10

10. Innovation is prized. 1 2 3 4 5 6 7 8 9 10

11. Appropriate knowledge management systems are in place. 1 2 3 4 5 6 7 8 9 10

12. Quality failure is acceptable. 1 2 3 4 5 6 7 8 9 10

TOTAL SCORE = _____

Figure 66: Adaptive Culture Audit.
Source: Alexander, 2001.

The Problem with Mergers and Acquisitions

Businesses of all types are looking at mergers and acquisitions (M&As). For example, non-consulting IT companies across the spectrum are seeking to build up their consulting operations, and M&As are seen as one of the top options. Issues such as changing laws, concerns over conflict of interest (audit versus consulting), and the e-flu have the leaders of high-tech professional services organizations considering any and all options (including M&As) to improve business viability.

Other services organizations of all shapes and sizes are in the same boat, looking for profitable ways to grow. Yet no matter the business rationale, the thought of blending one's own culture with that of another organization can be quite disturbing. People grow comfortable with the way things are. Perhaps your services business has been a profit center for years and the other organization has provided services for free or routinely provided deep discounts to close deals. Worse yet, their finance people might have established a ceiling on what percentage of the business should be dedicated to services—*No more than 40% of our business should be involved in services!* This is not an easy mindset to overcome.

Also consider these findings from another study: "55 to 77 percent of such deals (mergers and acquisitions) failed to deliver the organizational and/or financial results that were intended, and more than 50 percent of those failures are attributable to serious cultural incompatibility" (Healy, Krishna, and Ruback, 1992). Specifically talking about professional services firms, David Maister states that "Mergers can be successful—it's just that few of them have been" (Meister, 1997, p. 313). Sobering information. The first point is that one should seriously question the payoff from combining two or more distinct organizations: Does the potential value far outweigh the cost, hassle, and risk of the venture? Management thought leader Gary Hamel (2000) thinks that mergers and acquisitions are just desperate actions intended to cover up the mistakes of poor management. If two dinosaurs mate, all you end up with is a really big dinosaur.

Nevertheless, if one decides to move along this joining path, then it is clear one needs to strongly consider the cultural fit before taking action. No prudent businessperson would consider a takeover or major partnership without first undertaking due diligence. The evidence makes a strong case for organizations also to undertake a "cultural due diligence" as part of the exami-

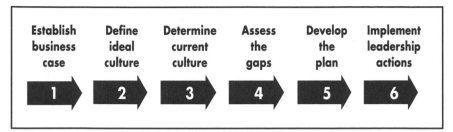

Figure 67: The six phases of culture change methodology.

nation process (Healy, Krishna, and Rubeck, 1992). As will be pointed out in the next section, it is very important for anyone contemplating a merger or acquisition to gain an in-depth understanding of *both* organizations before attempting the move.

Culture Change—Methodology to the Rescue

OK, now the tough part. We now know the importance of organization culture, what it is, its key characteristics, its dimensions and impact on strategy, the dark side of culture, the three core elements of any culture, and the special challenges of blending cultures. But how do we change our culture if we need to (which is virtually all of us)? How do we reinvent our culture if we are making the leap to s-business? Figure 67 shows a proven methodology that we've found successful in working with a variety of services organizations.*

Note: In most cases, culture change is only a part (although a very important part) of an entire transition process. This will be discussed in Chapter 10.

Note also that we are strong proponents of organizations making changes of any type actively involving as many individuals from the organization as possible in those changes. Involvement brings ownership—an essential catalyst for change. But keep in mind that while many change-related activities can be implemented very well without outside consultation, culture change is not one of them. Because culture by definition is ingrained into the fiber of an organization, it becomes invisible to anyone who is a member after only a few months. Therefore, it takes capable, outside eyes to view the culture as it really is and to assist the organization's leaders in assessing the changes needed and helping make them happen.

Phase One: Establish the Business Case for Culture Change

First understand and build a business case to answer the questions: Why now? Is our current culture inappropriate for our desired strategy? Will cultural blending take place (M&A) one way or another? Is our organization attempting to make the leap from a product-centered organization to s-business? Or is our culture so out of whack with what we need to do that it is hindering performance today and will probably be a major stumbling block tomorrow?

Culture change is challenging. Therefore a business case (including an understanding of the impact on performance of *not* changing), complete with cost-benefit analysis, must be in place and communicated to employees if the necessary efforts are to take place.

Phase Two: Define the Ideal S-Business Culture

Once your services strategy is in place, use three inputs (the three core elements, the cultural dimension scale, values of services leaders) to determine what your ideal culture would look like and feel like. First, ground your thinking in the three core elements of adaptive cultures and think through how people can embody these elements. Next, use the culture dimensions as a guide to shape the attributes that best align with the services strategy that you are pursuing. Finally, shape your preferred cultural future based upon the core values of the services leadership team. With these elements in place, you will have a high standard upon which to measure future actions.

Phase Three: Determine the Current Culture

Using document reviews, surveys, focus groups, interviews, and direct observation, determine what your services culture is today. Using the tools described earlier, you can quantify it according to the three core elements and the Cultural Dimension Scale. If you are making an s-business transition, you will also need to determine the current culture of the product-centered parts of your organization. If you are anticipating a merger or acquisition, you should examine the culture of the other organization as well. (For some tips on more informal ways to assess an organization, see the sidebar "The Quick and Dirty Guide to Cultural Assessment.")

Phase Four: **Assess the Gaps**

This phase along with Phase Five are best conducted in a facilitated, off-site session. It compares the ideal culture with the current culture to determine a realistic culture target for the

The Quick and Dirty Guide to Culture Assessment

We have outlined some sound and proven methods to conduct an organizational cultural assessment, including document analysis, focus groups, structured interviews, and expert observations. However, there are some more informal ways to help you make educated guesses. Every organization has hundreds of "indicators" as to what the organization is all about whatever vision statements or the annual report might espouse. Here are some straightforward places to look, listen, and question to learn these cultural clues. This information can be used to give you ideas about completing the two diagnostics.

Warning: Remember these are indicators. Just as crossing one's arms over one's chest might mean someone is cold rather than defiant, an office lined with big game trophies may mean an executive has borrowed an office and is not a winner-take-all kind of guy. Never use these tips alone without other analysis.

Look:

From the moment you drive up to your facility (global headquarters or local branch), start viewing this world with a fresh perspective and record the impact on your senses. What does the parking lot look like? Reserved spaces or first come first? How about customer and visitor parking—up front or around back? Employee of the month parking? Early or late is the parking lot full or empty?

What do you see in the reception area? How do you sign in? Are you treated like a criminal or an honored guest? Is there a friendly receptionist with a smile offering you coffee, or a phone with a list of vendor rules behind a plexiglass barrier? What is prominently displayed? Professional reprints of the latest PR efforts? History of the founder? What is emphasized?

Are the people you see smiling and in animated conversation? Do they greet you as they pass or offer to help if you have that "can't find the rest room look"? In conference rooms and working spaces, what is portrayed? The company's values? Quality methods? Slogans?

Do people work at open desks, in cubicles, or in private offices? Are office doors open or closed? Are people grouped by function or by work team? Is the environment orderly? What are people wearing—business attire or business casual?

What about meetings? Do they involve formal agendas, polite discussions with punctual endings, or haphazard sessions, with roaming dialogues? Are disagreements politely ignored or free-for-alls encouraged? What are the decision-making criteria? Do people look toward the big dog? Are issues argued on the merits of the facts or are emotions the drivers of what happens? Are decisions made quickly or slowly and deliberately?

What tools are people using? Laptops? Whiteboards? Notepads? Is everyone on the same type of Dell computer with the exact same version of Windows or do you see a few Macs around?

What is celebrated? Beating the competition on a big deal? Winning a quality award? How is it celebrated? A sit-down dinner or a Friday afternoon beer bust?

Dinner with the company president or a donation to the United Way?

Listen

Overall, is there a quiet hush like that found in library stacks, or is it more like the low-level hum of a NASA control room? Or is the main sound more like the pent up energy and occasional bursts of laughter at a boisterous wedding reception?

What about overheard individual conversations? Are they mainly outside-focused—a discussion on solving some customer problem? A debate on the merits of a new approach? Or are they inside-focused—griping about changes in the healthcare plan? Questioning what will happen as a result of the upcoming merger?

Feel

Close your eyes in different locations of the facility. What emotions come to mind? Comfortable or unfriendly? Warm or cold? Relaxed or stuffy? Formal or informal? Laid back or frenetic? Do you feel like staying or do you want to get out of there? Would your dog be welcome? Would you feel more at home wearing a blue suit or blue jeans?

near future. First identify areas of alignment as these are critical strengths that must stay the same and are the leverage points for change. Then identify the critical change points, dimensions of high importance with large gaps. The strength and importance of your leverage points and your critical change points will help you to determine (1) how significant the change will be, (2) how long it will take, and (3) what resources will be needed.

Phase Five: **Develop the Action Plan**

Here the services leadership team takes all the facts and determines the path toward change. The members of this team (although they have hopefully been involved through all four phases above) must address the business (and social, political, and personal) aspects of changing the culture. What are the risks? What are the odds of success? How "visible" should the culture change approach be? What is the leader's role in the transition? What type of investment will be required? How will success be measured? What milestones will keep the organization going along the right road? Answers to these questions include all the "who-what-whens" of any good plan.

Phase Six: Implementation: S-Business Leadership Actions

The success factors required for implementing culture change are no different than those necessary for implementing any major change initiative: sponsorship, measurable goals, action steps with ownership and completion dates, tracking, etc. Therefore, we will concentrate on the culture change implementation implications from the perspective of the services leader, and outline some suggested actions for champions of the cultural change:

1. *Accept the difficulty of the task.* Research looking at attempted culture change showed that in twenty-two cases of attempted cultural change, even the managers themselves (who tended to declare victory based on the slimmest of evidence) admitted that they had failed in sixteen of the cases (Wilkins, 1989). Resources, focus, and tenacity are called for.

2. *Do your homework.* As noted earlier, organizations almost always get in trouble when they quit listening to one or more groups of stakeholders. For the organization to even be willing to consider change, it needs a great deal of credible information that cannot be refuted. As we've suggested, internally conduct a culture audit. Externally, do market research. People can naysay each other, but it is hard to ignore the voice of the customer.

3. *Establish a sense of crisis.* Here successful leaders demonstrate that if change doesn't occur, and occur soon, some or all of the existing values of the current culture are at risk.

Remember, the more successful the organization has been in the past, the more challenging this assignment is.

4. *Create a new direction.* Culture change is appropriate only as a part of a larger organization change. Therefore, the new organization direction must be based on a services strategy appropriate to the cold, hard reality of the new marketplace. If successful, this can move the organization out of crisis for the near future. Simultaneously, to build a sustainable culture for the future (and avoid other crises), implementation of the new strategy needs to incorporate the behaviors associated with the three core elements of contribution, candor, and constant learning.

5. *Align support systems.* The new direction means that people are going to have to behave in different (sometimes radically different) ways than they have before. To overcome inertia, all support systems must be changed to expect, encourage, and reward the new behaviors while strongly discouraging operating in a business-as-usual mode. The emphasis should be on the creation and nurturing of the elements of contribution, candor, and constant learning. These three should become the central tenets of the new alignment. (By the way, how to do this must be thought through and be ready for implementation before the crisis and the need for change are announced.)

6. *Inform and involve.* This is the mantra of services leaders, as they tell and explain and preach the new gospel of the new organization, including its rationale and how the change will positively impact all stakeholders. Furthermore, smart leaders involve as many people as possible in the process to get them to take personal ownership of the change.

7. *Constantly communicate.* Effective leaders know that to truly communicate a new concept means multiple messages delivered in multiple ways. Whatever the format, these elements should be included: why the culture must change, what will stay the same, what will be different, how success will be measured, and what's in it for everybody.

> Genius of Einstein
> Vision of Jefferson
> Strength of Superman
> Patience of Gandhi
> Communications skills of Roosevelt
> Creativity of da Vinci
> Magnanimity of Sister Teresa
> Ambition of the Clintons
> The conviction of Churchill—never, never give up!

Figure 68: Ideal attributes of the s-business champion.

8. *Walk the talk.* Everyone will be watch the top dogs to see if this is just another flavor of the month or serious business. Senior management must walk the talk and even go out of its way to reward new behaviors that align with the desired culture shift, and to punish behaviors (particularly of managers) that violate stated principles. Nothing indicates commitment more than the firing a few managers that "don't get it."

The Ideal Attributes of S-Business Leaders Embarking on Culture Change

We have studied and worked in the culture change space for many years and finally have come up with the ultimate list of ideal attributes of the s-business champion for you to carry around in your wallet and refer to when things get really tough as you focus on culture change. They are shown in Figure 68. The "genius of Einstein," the "vision of Jefferson," the "strength of Superman," and so on may be a little tongue-in-cheek. However, we believe you get the picture. Hard work, coupled with honing your skills and perseverance, are critical components of the s-business champion.

Conclusion

Organization culture is a major contributor to organization success or failure. By its very nature, it can prove to be resilient to needed change. However, well-informed leaders of services organizations with the will to change can help create effective s-business cultures that are strong, adaptive, and sustainable over time. The results of these high-performance cultures are both excellent stakeholder value and exceptional financial performance.

Chapter 10

Transitioning from "Business-as-Usual" to "Business-as-Exceptional": Creating Top-Performing S-Businesses

RESEARCH FACTOID: "Get your marketing right" was the number one recommended priority by those who had most successfully made the transition to s-business.

PONDER POINT: About three out of four major change efforts fail to achieve and sustain the desired change objectives.

PURPOSE: This chapter will show you what it takes to undergo major s-transition by:

- Explaining the special challenges of s-business transition
- Demonstrating the principles to be followed in guiding major change
- Providing a three-phase transition framework
- Sharing the best practices required to make it happen

"Yes!" you say, "I am now a believer." The evidence is overwhelming and now you want to transform your organization to a high-performance s-business. What are the benchmarks? What are the best practices? What are the steps to successfully transitioning from today's business-as-usual to tomorrow's s-business?

Not so fast....There's a cold, hard reality out there. The troubling truth of the matter is that about three out of four major change efforts fail to achieve and sustain the desired objectives. Our own experience in advising organizations confirms this, and probably your personal experience does, as well. Think back over the last few years during times you experienced the launching of initiatives such as Six Sigma, Process Reengineering, or Balanced Scorecard. How many of those efforts have brought about the lasting value intended at the time of announcement?

Obstacles to Change

Shortly, we will introduce the best practices of s-business change (s-change) implementation. However, before talking about what to do, it is important to ponder what not to do. Ten common obstacles that pop up time and again when organizations (and the people who compose them) attempt to do things differently can be seen in Figure 69. (See also the sidebar, "But

Figure 69: Why changes don't produce change.
Source: Based on Ulrich, 1997.

1. Not tied to strategy
2. Seen as a fad or quick fix
3. Short-term perspective
4. Change undermined by political realities
5. Grandiose expectations versus simple successes
6. Inflexible change designs
7. Lack of leadership regarding change
8. Lack of measurable, tangible results
9. Fear of the unknown
10. Inability to mobilize commitment to sustain change

But We Already Know Our Customers!

Many times, organization leaders assume they understand customer needs, new buyer behaviors, and emerging marketplace requirements. They assure us that although they have never done any specific services market research they have all the information they need to make sound business decisions. Baloney!

The same people who, rationally enough, wouldn't consider buying a personal car without a dozen hours of research will make go/no go decisions on services businesses based upon their intuition. Even executives with strong services business histories can be blindsided, as the pace of change continues to speed up and what was hard fact six months ago is past history today. It is just bad business not to consistently conduct on-going, in-depth market research, especially during the s-business ramp-up years.

We Already Know Our Customers" for a slightly different perspective on this problem.) Recognize any of them? We don't believe further elaboration is required. Needless to say, all must be recognized, and steps need to be put in place to deal with each of them. However, in addition to these ten obstacles, there are some special challenges to transitioning to s-business that must be considered before embarking on the journey of change.

Special Challenges of S-Change

As already noted a time or two, big-time change (targeted at making major improvements in organization performance) is tough. Yet making the transition to s-business is often more difficult by an order of magnitude. Two factors drive this.

The first factor is the extreme difference between the two types of offerings of traditional businesses and s-businesses. The products produced by traditional organizations can easily be seen, felt, and described. However, the offerings of s-businesses (services and professional services) are intangible. The challenge of dealing with the added complexity of intangibility alone raises the bar. In addition, as pointed out in the Introduction, production, quality control, customer interaction, etc., must be viewed quite differently in a services business compared to a product company. These distinctions have a fundamental impact on how one produces, markets, sells, delivers, services, and measures the performance of s-business products and the success of the s-business itself. What may have worked extremely well in managing a traditional product-based organization will be ineffective in the world of s-business. Hence, different characteristics and competencies in people must be sought, different management support systems created, and different metrics evaluated to reward performance and guide the enterprise. All of this is further complicated because, in most cases, organizations that have made the transition to an s-business orientation still produce and sell the same goods they did before the transition. This is a significant management challenge.

The second factor compounding the difficulty of s-business transition deals with organization culture. Whether a management consultancy, a bank, a software producer, or a heavy machine manufacturer, the principles and practices of Total Quality or Process Improvement ring true—there is a strong element of common sense built into these models that people can readily relate to. Who can be against quality? Who would not want to eliminate waste? And though it is difficult, people inside the organization at all levels can accept the tenets of the proposed new way of doing things over time. Furthermore, with some modifications to the management system, the organization eventually can integrate these types of initiatives into the culture. But not so with s-business. As stated in Chapter 9, culture abhors attempts to change it and will do whatever it can to maintain the status quo. S-business is a full frontal attack on the existing culture, and the defensive culture mechanisms of the organization will resist any way they can. The fundamental problem is that, in most cases, the people running the show got there by being exceptionally good at making, marketing, selling, delivering, and servicing products. Products are their expertise, and this expertise got them promoted. Their past successes (built around products) helped create, develop, and nurture the culture—a culture that lives, breathes, and reinforces goods-related success while shunning other alternatives to business. In this setting, services were necessary evils tolerated because they were a requirement in supporting products. Service was traditionally a cost center and services were things negotiated and often given away either to make a sale or to keep a customer happy. S-business requires a serious flip-flop in thinking. Services now must be viewed as the principal products of the organization, the true value-adders, the potential differentiators in the marketplace, and the keys to profitable revenue. Executives now must view products as customers have for a long time—as commodities that take a secondary role in a Total Solutions package. This is not an easy transition to make, as it flies directly in the face of the tried and true. So the truth of the matter is that the very things that made an organization successful yesterday are the same things that hinder its success today. Bringing about this s-business mindshift is a leadership challenge of the highest order.

Leading Change

So how does one prepare for the tension that develops and the resistance that naturally occurs when the people of the organization are asked to behave in new and different ways? How does one deal with the immediate drop in productivity as water cooler conversations (both face-to-face and via electronic media) speculating on the impact and political ramifications of the change and the always present "What's going to happen to me?" kind of question take priority over the mundane tasks of meeting customer requirements?

Here are a few proven concepts and one powerful tool that s-business champions can use for overcoming the resistance to the transition, steps that if followed can help lower fears, knock down barriers, and smooth the change by getting key people onboard quickly (Alexander and Hordes, 2002).

Managing change and the natural resistance that occurs means addressing each of the *four fundamental elements* that are the drivers of how well and how fast people do what you want them to do:

1. *Constancy.* Fear of change (the unknown) affects everyone, so don't emphasize it! In communicating change efforts, *start* by explaining and reinforcing what *won't change*. These include the organization's values that will remain constant, the elements of the strategy that will stay the same, and the aspects of people's jobs that will continue to be the same. This approach helps ground people and give them the feeling of control required to deal with what must be different. It also greatly increases people's willingness to listen. Our recommended communication pattern for each element of a change is:

   1. State what remains constant.
   2. Explain what will change, why it will change, and the stakeholder benefits of the change.
   3. Explain what the organization is doing to support the change.

   Here is a simple example of a communication strategy regarding the compensation package for a product salesperson being asked to actively sell services:

   - *Constant:* Compensation for product sales will stay the same. ("We are not taking anything away from you.")
   - *Change:* There will be additional compensation for selling services. ("You can only gain from this.")
   - *Support:* Training in selling services will be provided. ("We know that you need new knowledge and skills—we are willing to invest in you to do the new job.")

   Having worked with transitioning many a product sales organization to selling services, believe us, the above approach is a must!

2. *Predictability.* This is also important in managing change. Professionals need to fully understand not only what is going

to occur but when it will happen. This allows people to schedule their own actions and get themselves psychologically ready to meet the new challenges. In our product salesperson example above, predictability can be established by immediately sharing the key points of the new services compensation while simultaneously scheduling the salespeople for their first training session.

3. *Personal absorption.* The comfort levels required here need to be considered because people can manage only so much change at one time. At the most, an organization's threshold for change at any given time is three major initiatives. However, an individual's personal threshold is only one, and each person varies as to the amount of time they need to go through each change phase. A good way to determine if the pace of change is on track is to conduct some focus groups with affected staff members and ask how they are managing the change and what more can be done to help them absorb what is occurring. Sometimes simple things like communications updates, reviews of time lines, and personal visits with functional change agents and sponsors can help. Lunch and Learn sessions to find out how everything is moving along help as well. With our above-mentioned product sales force, the best way to check on personal absorption is to accompany some salespeople in the field for a few days, observing them making sales calls to actually see performance then asking them about their comfort level with the new expectations.

4. *Level of resolve.* Following the above steps is often adequate in most situations. However, when individuals are being asked to make major changes in behavior, their own personal resolve becomes an important success factor. Personal resolve is fortified by first understanding that one will be personally affected by change, like it or not, then thinking through the options, implications, and actions. Providing training on change fundamentals and how each person can deal with changes on personal and professional levels helps increase people's resolve to effectively manage the change. Our product sales example is

one of these situations, as it involves a major change and many salespeople are at risk of not successfully transitioning. Along with the absolutely necessary selling services training focusing on knowledge and skills, there should be facilitated sessions dealing with the mindset issues associated with this significant transition.

The Motivation to Change Matrix

Dealing across the board with the four elements described above will have very positive results. However, in any change worth doing, there will be specific pockets of resistance—some involving key stakeholders critical to the transition.

One tool that has worked well for our firm in helping our clients make the s-business transition, is the Motivation to Change Matrix (Figure 70). It is a simple, but extremely helpful, tool in helping one to quickly size up the motivation level of all the key stakeholders related to supporting or resisting the change. Here is a brief description of these four classifications found in the diagram:

1. *Resistors:* Those in the organization that you believe will actively work at stopping the change and maintaining the status quo.

2. *Let it Happen People:* Individuals who are neutral to the change and will neither support nor try to stop the transformation. "Que sera sera" is the motto of these folks.

3. *Help it Happen People:* These are the people who are willing to dedicate some percentage of their time to help move the change effort forward.

4. *Make it Happen People:* These are the highly valued change sponsors who have the capability and the desire to help push the rock up hill. Their philosophy is "We will do whatever it takes to make the transition successful."

Once having figured out where each of the key stakeholders are located on the matrix, the next step is to create a tactical plan for each quadrant. Brainstorming helps generate ideas on first

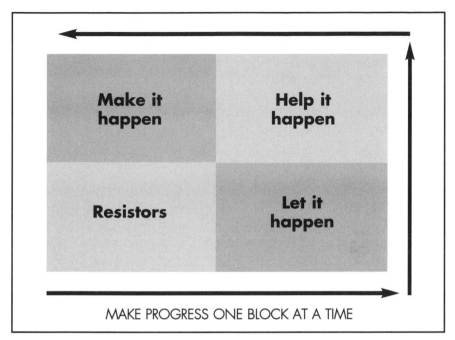

Figure 70: The Motivation to Change Matrix.
Source: Adapted from Pannone, Wimby, and Woolf, 1985.

finding out what is important to these stakeholders then coming up with interesting ways to address them. First start with the "Make it Happen People" and try to leverage their desire to bring about change. The tactic for each of the other three quadrants is to move them along, one quadrant at a time. For example, forget about turning "Resistors" into sponsors. Just try and neutralize them by moving them into the "Let It Happen" zone.

Here is a personal example. In one circumstance, a divisional manager was quite vocal about not supporting the s-business change until we discovered that the root cause of his resistance was that it was not his idea. The strategy developed to move him into the "Let it Happen" box was as simple as developing an internal news story with his picture on the front cover along with an interview in which he was given credit for the s-business change. Later we found out that most people believed that the s-business transformation was his idea. Consequently, his attitude and motivation changed quickly. Although he never lifted a finger to support the project, he no longer tried to stop it either. The project proceeded on course and was ultimately quite successful. Remember, keep brainstorming how to move everyone up at least one notch.

Managing the Transition

The previous section provided a conceptual framework and an important tool to personally lead change. This section will explain the actual transition process and the steps needed to carry it out. Although we have demonstrated the challenges of s-business transition, hundreds of organizations have made a successful transformation. Just as we know the things that thwart the movement to s-business, we also know the best practices to follow in making the transition successful. As shown in Figure 71, there are three phases that can smooth and ease a successful implementation.

Figure 71: The transition to s-business.

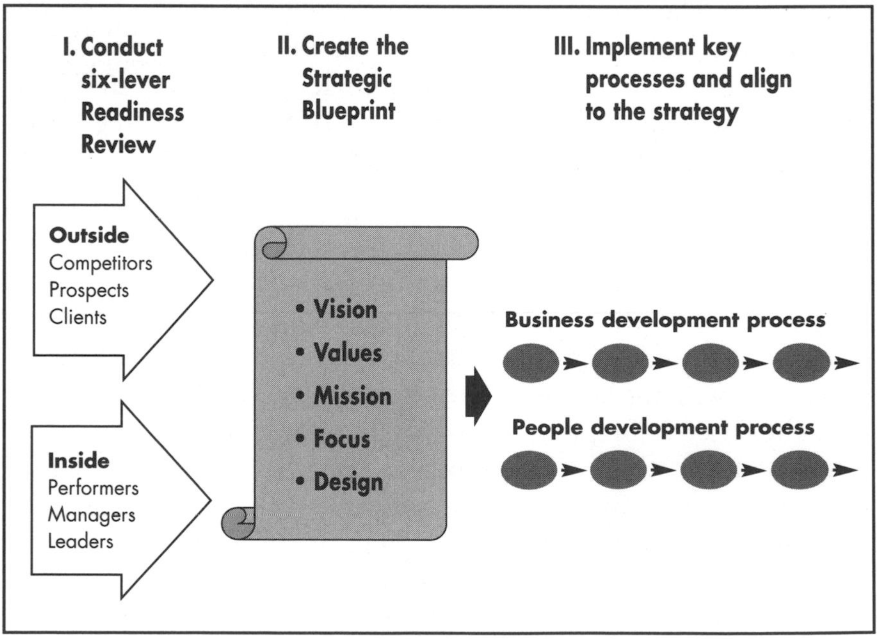

Phase One: **Conduct a Readiness Review**

The Readiness Review is the absolutely vital first step in making significant s-business changes. This frank evaluation determines an organization's current s-performance and s-readiness, allowing the leadership to make decisions based upon facts, not guesses. Done well it acts as a reality check, a prioritizer of issues, an identifier of high-potential levers, and an involver of key stakeholders who need to be supporters (or at least "Let It Happen" people when the actual changes are implemented). The Readiness Review should do the following:

- Confirm or question assumptions, objectives, and plans
- Determine the size of the performance gap
- Compare performance against best s-practices
- Ascertain the likelihood of overall success (sometimes a go/no go decision)
- Establish priorities (low-hanging fruit and leverage points)
- Enhance credibility both outside and inside the organization
- Build a business case to take the services to the next level

The Readiness Review is two-dimensional. It looks outside to uncover strengths and weaknesses in the services the organization already provides, comparing this performance to customer expectations, needs, and competitive positions. It looks inside to gain critical information from the leaders, managers, and performers of the organization to determine the size of the services gap and the realistic probability of the organization's ability to close that gap. Included in this audit should be a review of the management systems, people capabilities, and culture analysis. The six success levers become the framework from which to compare and contrast desired performance with current reality. Below are the types of questions it will help to answer:

- *Strategy:* What is the most appropriate s-business strategy — one that will help drive the overall organization mission and focus most effectively? What is the current services value proposition? Is it appropriate? Are goals realistic or not challenging enough?

- *Marketing:* What is the market message? How well has this been communicated? How credible is the services organization seen in the marketplace? Should the services organization attempt to build its own brand, to co-brand, or to make its brand "seamless," integrating all products and services under one roof? How well do current services offerings align with current needs? What is the competitive position? What is being offered that customers don't value highly? Can these be eliminated or offered through less costly means? What are the emerging needs that have the potential for differentiation and higher margins?

- *Selling:* How effectively and efficiently are services offerings being sold? What can be done to improve product sales performance in selling services? How can the power of the services providers be leveraged to enhance business development efforts?

- *Delivering:* What can be done to enhance delivery productivity? How up-to-the-task are the services providers?

- *Operations:* What is the existing leverage model? Can it be improved? How robust is the knowledge management system? What improvements can be made?

- *Talent:* How well are star performers recruited, hired, developed, and retained? What changes can be made to improve performance overall?

Answering these questions will provide reams of important information. The Readiness Review will yield an overall score on each of the six factors, as the example in Figure 72 shows. Furthermore, specific data covering all the questions above will be uncovered.

Many tools can be helpful in conducting the Readiness Review and analyzing the results. However, one in particular is especially powerful in identifying reality versus wishes: the Customer Viewpoint Matrix (Figure 73). Using hard customer data gathered in the Readiness Review, this tool plots out where customers see an organization's offerings today as well as the

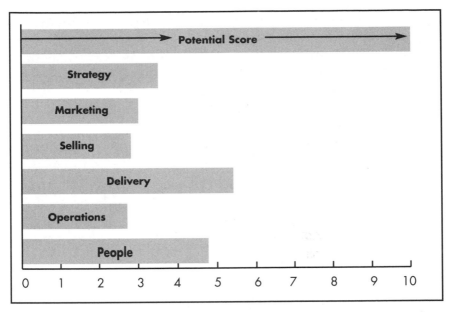

Figure 72: Readiness Review summary results high level: example.

Figure 73: The Customer Viewpoint Matrix: current services performance.

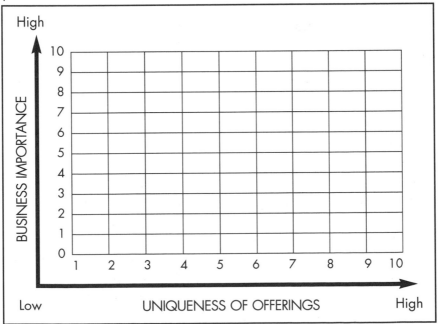

offerings of its best competitor. This tells management at a glance the appropriateness of the company's services strategy, its competitive position, and the opportunities for competitive advantage. These findings will help lead the discussion around strategy to be held later in the blueprinting session.

GATHERING INFORMATION

Our personal preference in conducting Readiness Reviews is that (1) they be balanced between quantitative and qualitative methods, (2) they have an element of expert observation, and (3) the research team be made up of both outside professional researchers and managers *and* executives of the organization.

1. Quantitative research methods are important, but qualitative one-on-one interviews and focus groups allow the investigators to go beyond surface responses to gain information that is both "rich" and "thick," providing the rationale behind answers and deeper insights. For the complex issues of services, this is a must. Furthermore, if done correctly, the information collected in personal meetings with clients and customers can suggest high-potential new services offerings, shifts in existing needs, and services line integration issues, as well as current gaps where the client is looking for some assistance and help. A good balance of quantitative and qualitative approaches yields the highest-quality results.

2. People sometimes don't do what they say they do. That's not because they are evil or pathological liars, it is just that they don't know what they do and instead of fessing up they tell you what they think you want to hear. Hence, trying to understand existing skill levels and estimating performance gaps related to selling or delivering services through interview and focus groups is worse than useless. The only way to get a true grasp of this is through field observation of the current (or potential) sellers and providers of services by services pros trained in observation research. Without this element of the assessment, the study findings will be questionable.

3. Outside researchers can add professionalism to the information-gathering process coupled with solid analytic support. However, since research reports too often gather dust on management shelves, steps should be taken to motivate action. Getting executives to step up to the plate to interview a cross section of the organization's best customers not only goes a long way in demonstrating a commitment to partnership and continuing a strong relationship with the clients/customers, but also helps gain the buy-in and commitment of these execs for making positive changes. This is a powerful tool in building confidence in the research findings and creating urgency to take action.

Phase Two: Create the Strategic Blueprint

The second phase in the transition process is to organize an off-site meeting with executives and other key stakeholders. The goal of this type of meeting is to create a high-level strategic roadmap, complete with a focus on building the organization's services practice. Having seasoned professional services consultants (ideally the same folks who helped conduct the Readiness Review) help design and facilitate the meeting is worth the investment. In addition to keeping everyone on target, consultants can provide an outside perspective on where the organization's market is headed as well as provide feedback on the reality specific to the company's strategic services plan.

Using the information gathered in the Readiness Review, the best thinking of the assembled leadership team, and the methods and processes designed by the Strategic Blueprint facilitators, this session allows participants to do the following:

- Collegially discuss issues, challenges, and opportunities involved in a successful transition
- Ponder options and their potential impacts
- Generate a realistic yet motivational direction for the services organization, plus create a map on how to get there

- Create a "market story" that highlights the uniqueness of the services organization based upon what was learned from the Readiness Review
- Reach agreement on critical actions, timelines, and personal responsibilities

The benefits of this session include the following:

- Developing consensus through involvement
- Improving decisions by tapping the best thinking of key players
- Creating a common destiny for the management team
- Identifying any "management gaps " associated with hindering the change process
- Providing the vehicle for potential innovation
- Reaching agreement on common, consistent messages for all stakeholders, including what's in it for them
- Compressing the commitment cycle of the management team to the change

Keep in mind that the strategy session is a bit like navigating a ship through rocky waters. To successfully come through it with a high degree of satisfaction, a combination of elements and processes must come together: solid research, excellent facilitator skills, an open mind to challenging assumptions, and the ability to place one's bets in the right areas to leverage existing services or to break new ground.

Phase Three: **Define Core Processes**

The shift to s-business requires different expectations, different objectives, different tools, different processes and procedures, different reward systems, different everything. All the elements of people management have to be rethought before implementation begins. *Only* after conducting a Readiness Review and mapping out the new Strategic Blueprint is it time to address the elements that impact how people work. The most effective way to think through and act is to address the processes most important to any services business, the Business Development and People Development processes outlined in earlier chapters.

Helping Factors	Hindering Factors
Acceptance of new realities	Marketing challenges
Being customer-driven	Sales performance/mindset
Quality services personnel	Lack of talent
Making a strategy/culture shift	External factors
Changes on the product side	Competition from the product side

Figure 74: Crossing the chasm to s-business: top performer assessment.

Source: Alexander, 2002.

Crossing the Chasm

In conducting the s-business research referred to throughout this book (Alexander, 2002), leaders who had successfully made the transition to s-business were asked about their biggest helping factors and hindering factors in making this journey. Displayed in Figure 74 are the most common responses, ranked in order. Starting with the helping factors, getting key people to accept the new business realities of the services potential (better growth opportunities and margin potential) topped the list. Once people start to accept this fact, the wheels of change start to turn. "Being customer-driven" doesn't refer directly to the old cliché so often repeated in customer service circles. In this situation it has special significance, referring to basing the organizational strategy on the customer reality found in the Readiness Review and not the best guesses of former thinking. "Quality services personnel" refers to already having in place a core of top-notch services professionals, people who stepped up to the plate to lead and develop others in the organization. "Making a strategy/culture shift" was also a key helping factor, as top performers realized that this transition was a cultural one and addressed it as such. Finally, "Changes on the product side" (e.g., lack of proprietary products, pressures on growth and profitability, or stiff new competition) were seen as positive as product chieftans were more open to new ideas when the old guard was under attack.

On the hindrance side, "Marketing challenges" topped the list. The main factors here included lack of recognition in the marketplace, an unclear services concept, a weak services brand, and inadequate funding for services marketing. A close second challenge to making the transition was the "Sales performance/mindset." Two themes prevailed: the lack of capabilities required to sell services effectively, and the "product mentality" of the sales team.

As the grouping title suggests, comments in the "Lack of talent" category all revolved around not having enough qualified people. The elements of the "External factors" category included "recessive economy," "the reliability of new products," and "services consolidation." Finally, the "Competition from the product side" outlined the internal struggle proponents of a strong services initiative faced from those people in the organization who were pro-product.

Top Performer Recommendations

Also as a part of the s-business study (Alexander, 2002), participants in this series of transition questions provided whatever answers they wanted to the question "What recommendations (lessons learned) do you have for others moving to a services-driven business that are not as far along the transition path?" Figure 75 shows the clustered responses, ranked by order of their mention. Not surprisingly, the two top recommendations align with the two biggest hindering factors: marketing and sales. Under "Get your marketing right" were suggestions such as "create a clear service concept," "develop a strong customer value proposition," "focus on the basic services offerings first," and "establish budgets for marketing and branding." Under "Selling services is different," advice ranged from "hire a separate sales force" to "train the product sales force but move them

1. Get your marketing right
2. Selling services is different
3. Focus on the customer
4. Have a personal strategy
5. Manage the product side
6. Get top talent
7. Flawlessly deliver

Figure 75: Top performer recommendations.
Source: Alexander, 2002.

out if they don't perform" to "call at a higher level than the sales organization is accustomed." "Focus on the customer" meant understanding, caring for, and delivering on customer needs and expectations. "Have a personal strategy" included "create a plan and implement it every day," "learn from those who have gotten it right," "focus on quality," "be flexible," and "keep trucking." "Manage the product side" meant constantly tracking and communicating the value of the services element to the key stakeholders in the business. "Get top talent" and "Flawlessly deliver" are (hopefully) self-explanatory.

Conclusion

Managing the transition to exceptional services performance is challenging, but it's not rocket science. Understanding a leadership framework, following a proven model, and listening to the voices of those who have already made the journey can yield major rewards in a relatively short period of time. For most organizations the time for s-business is now!

References and Notes

Introduction

Alexander, James A. 2002. *The State of S-Business: An International Report of Progress, Performance and Best Practices.* Ft. Myers, FL: AFSM International.

Gummesson, Evert. 1999. *Total Relationship Marketing: Rethinking Marketing Management from 4Ps to 30Rs.* Woburn, MA: Butterworth–Heinemann.

Schwartz, M. H. 1992. What do the words "product" and "service" really mean for management? *Quality Progress, 25,* 6 (June), 35–39.

Zemke, Ron. 1992. The emerging art of service management. *Training, 29,* 1 (January), 36–42

Notes:

- About 90% of the "What's So Different About Services?" section was pulled directly from: Alexander, James, A. 1996. Managing products by intangibility and customer familiarity. *The Professional Journal* (AFSM International), *21,* 3 (December), 36–41.

- Throughout this book, the term *s-business research* always refers to the Alexander, 2002, study listed above.

Chapter 1

Alexander, James A. 2002. *The State of S-Business: An International Report of Progress, Performance and Best Practices.* Ft. Myers, FL: AFSM International.

Brown, Stephen W., Van Bennekom, Fred, Goffin, Keith, Hahn, Al, and Alexander, James A. 2001. S-business: Defining the services industry. White paper, Ft Myers, FL: AFSM International.

Notes:

- About 60% of this chapter was taken directly from: Alexander, James A., and Hordes, Mark. 2002. Building your s-business strategy for maximal organizational success. *Sbusiness* (AFSM International), *26*, 7 (March/April), 25–27.
- The remaining 40% of the chapter is based on the s-business research described in Alexander, 2002.

Chapter 2

Alexander, James A. 2000. *The State of High-Tech Professional Services: An Industry in Transition.* Ft. Myers. FL: AFSM International.

Alexander, James A. 2002. *The State of S-Business: An International Report of Progress, Performance and Best Practices.* Ft Myers, FL: AFSM International.

Note: 100% of this chapter is based directly on Alexander, 2002.

Chapter 3

Alexander, James A. 2002. *The State of S-Business: An International Report of Progress, Performance and Best Practices.* Ft. Myers, FL: AFSM International.

Note: The sections "Who Buys" and "Buying Strategy" were adapted from: Rackham, Neil, and De Vincentis, John. 1999. *Rethinking the Sales Force: Redefining Selling to Create and Capture Customer Value.* New York, NY: McGraw–Hill.

Chapter 4

Alexander, James A. 1995. Expanding the service business: 10 Steps to profitable professional services marketing. (Lecture handout.). AFSMI 2nd Pacific Rim Conference and Exposition (Sydney, Australia, March 27).

Alexander, James A. 1996. High-performance marketing: Managing products by intangibility and customer familiarity. *The Professional Journal* (AFSM International), *21*, 3 (December), 36–41.

Alexander, James A. 2000. *The State of High-Tech Professional Services: An Industry in Transition.* Ft. Myers, FL: AFSM International.

Alexander, James A. 2002. *The State of S-Business: An International Report of Progress, Performance and Best Practices.* Ft. Myers, FL: AFSM International.

Alexander, James A., and Hordes, Mark. 2002. Creating a truly remarkable professional services market approach: Six steps to success. *Professional Services Leadership Review* (AFSM International), second quarter, 1–7.

Alexander, James A., and Lyons, Michael C. 1995. *The Knowledge-Based Organization: Four Steps to Increasing Sales, Profits, and Market Share.* Chicago, IL: Irwin Professional Publishing.

Ames, B. Charles, and Hlavacek, James D. 1989. *Market Driven Management: Prescriptions for Survival in a Turbulent World.* Chicago, IL: Dow–Jones–Irwin.

Berry, Leonard L., and Parsuraman, A. 1991. *Marketing Services: Competing through Quality.* New York, NY: The Free Press.

Cespedes, Frank V. 1994. Industrial marketing: Managing new requirements. *Sloan Management Review, 35,* 3 (Spring), 36–45.

Donath, Bob. 1992. The customer as consultant. *Sales and Marketing Management*, *144*, 11 (September), 19–84.

Drucker, Peter F. 1995. *Managing in a Time of Great Change.* New York, NY: NAL Dutton.

Drucker, Peter F. 1996. Flashes of genius. *Inc.*, June, p. 79.

Martin, Justin. 1995. Ignore your customer. *Fortune*, May 1, p. 4.

McQuarrie, Edward F., and McIntyre, Shelby H. 1990. *Implementing the Marketing Concept Through a Program of Customer Visits.* MSI Report No. 90–107. Cambridge, MA: Marketing Science Institute.

Peters, Tom. 1995. Do it now, stupid! *Forbes ASAP*, August 28.

Prahalad, C. K., and Hamel, G. 1990. The core competencies of the corporation. *Harvard Business Review*, *68*, 3 (May/June), 79–91.

Quinn, J. B. 1992. *Intelligent Enterprise: A Knowledge and Service Based Paradigm for Industry.* New York, NY: The Free Press.

Reichheld, Frederick F. 1996. *The Loyalty Effect: The Hidden Force Behind Growth, Profits, and Lasting Value.* Boston, MA: Harvard Business School Press.

Reichheld, Frederick F., and Sasser, Earl W., Jr. 1990. Zero defections: Quality comes to services. *Harvard Business Review*, *68*, 5 (September/October), 105–111.

Robert, Michel. 1995. *Product Innovation Strategy: How Winning Companies Outpace Their Competitors.* New York, NY: McGraw–Hill.

Stalk, George, Jr., and Hout, Thomas M. 1990. *Competing Against Time: How Time-Based Competition Is Reshaping Global Markets.* New York, NY: The Free Press.

Whiteley, Richard, and Hessan, Diane. 1996. *Customer Centered Growth: Five Proven Strategies for Building Competitive Advantage.* Reading, MA: Addison–Wesley.

Notes:

- "The Services Marketing Challenge" section is 70% taken from Alexander, 1996.

- The "Services Marketing Principles" section is 95% taken from Alexander, 1996.
- The "Services Portfolio Management" section is 50% taken from Alexander, 1996.

Chapter 5

Alexander, James A. 1996. High-performance marketing: Managing products by intangibility and customer familiarity. *The Professional Journal* (AFSM International), *21*, 3 (December), 36–41.

Alexander, James A. 2000. *The State of High-Tech Professional Services: An Industry in Transition.* Ft. Myers, FL: AFSM International.

Alexander, James A. 2001. Sales quality: Getting better sales faster. *The Professional Journal* (AFSM International), 25, 10 (May), 56–57.

Alexander, James A., and Hordes, Mark. 2002a. S-business: The global mandate. *Sbusiness* (AFSM International), *26*, 6 (January/February), 43–44.

Alexander, James A., and Hordes, Mark. 2002b. The ten commandments of selling professional services. *Professional Services Leadership Report* (AFSM International), first quarter, 5–14.

Alexander, James A., and Lyons, Michael. 1995. *The Knowledge-Based Organization: Four Steps to Increasing Sales, Profits, and Market Share.* Chicago, IL: Irwin Professional Publishing.

Gilbert, Thomas F. 1979. *Human Competence: Engineering Worthy Performance.* New York, NY: McGraw–Hill.

Hordes, Mark. 2001. Best day, everyday: Rules of the road for "getting to yes" in professional services selling. *The Professional Journal* (AFSM International), 25, 6 (January), 46–49.

Kennedy Information Research Group. 1999. Few clients "very satisfied" with consultants. *Consultants News* (Kennedy Information), *29*, 11 (November), 12.

Levitt, Theodore. 1981. Marketing intangible products and product intangibles. *Harvard Business Review*, *58*, May/June, 83–89.

Note: This chapter was taken 90% from Alexander and Hordes, 2002b.

Chapter 6

Gilbert, Thomas F. 1978. *Human Competence: Engineering Worthy Performance*. New York, NY: McGraw–Hill.

Kennedy Information Research Group. 1999. Few clients "very satisfied" with consultants. *Consultants News* (Kennedy Information), *29*, 11 (November), 12.

Chapter 7

Alexander, James A. 1999. Knowledge management. *The Professional Journal* (AFSM International), *24*, 5 (December), 11–12.

Alexander, James A. 2001. Sales quality: Getting better sales faster. *The Professional Journal* (AFSM International), *25*, 10 (May), 56–57.

Hansen, Morten T., Nohria, Nitin, and Tierney, Thomas. 1999. What's your strategy for managing knowledge? *Harvard Business Review*, 77, 2 (March/April), 106–116.

Maister, D. H. 1993. *Managing the Professional Service Firm*. New York, NY: The Free Press.

Parasuraman, A., Zeithaml, Valeria A., and Berry, Leonard I. 1985. A conceptual model of service quality and its implications for future research. *Journal of Marketing* (American Marketing Association), *49*, Fall, 41–50.

Chapter 8

Alexander, James A. 1999a. Managing knowledge workers. *The Professional Journal* (AFSM International), *24*, 1 (August), 48–50.

Alexander, James A. 1999b. A test of a rapid developer model. In K. P. Kuchinke (Ed.), *1999 Conference Proceedings, Academy of Human Resource Development*, pp. 520–528. Baton Rouge, LA: Academy of Human Resource Development.

Alexander, James A. 2002. *The State of S-Business: An International Report of Progress, Performance and Best Practices.* Ft. Myers, FL: AFSM International.

Harnish, Verne. 2002. *Mastering the Rockefeller Habits.* New York, NY: SelectBooks.

Watson Wyatt. 2001. *Watson Wyatt's Human Capital Index® 2001/2002 Survey Report: Human Capital As a Lead Indicator of Shareholder Value.* Washington, DC: Watson Wyatt Worldwide.

Note: The "Managing Knowledge-Workers in an S-Business" section is 95% taken from Alexander, 1999a.

Chapter 9

Alexander, James A. 1999. A test of a rapid developer model. In K. P. Kuchinke (Ed.), *1999 Conference Proceedings, Academy of Human Resource Development*, pp. 520–528. Baton Rouge, LA: Academy of Human Resource Development.

Alexander, James A. 2001. Creating high-performance culture: Leadership roles and responsibilities. *Professional Services Leadership Review* (AFSM International), fourth quarter, 5–9.

Andersen Consulting. n.d. Strategy research (source unknown).

Argyris, C., and Schön, D. A. 1996. *Organizational Learning II.* Reading, MA: Addison–Wesley.

Burke, W. W., and Litwin, G. 1989. A causal model of organizational performance. In J. W. Pfeiffer (Ed.), *The 1989 Annual: Developing Human Resources*. San Diego, CA: University Associates.

Hamel, G. 2000. *Leading the Revolution*. Boston, MA: Harvard Business School Press.

Hampton–Turner, Charles. 1992. *Creating Corporate Culture: From Discord to Harmony*. Reading, MA: Addison–Wesley.

Healy, P. M., Palepu, Krishna G., and Ruback, S. R. 1992. Does corporate performance improve after mergers? *Journal of Financial Economics, 31*, 2 (April), 135–175.

Kotter, J. P., and Heskett, J. L. 1992. *Corporate Culture and Performance*. New York, NY: The Free Press.

Maister, D. H. 1997. *True Professionalism*. New York, NY: The Free Press.

Schein, E. J. 1992. *Organizational Culture and Leadership*, 2nd ed. San Francisco, CA: Jossey–Bass.

Wilkins, A. L. 1989. *Developing Corporate Character*. San Francisco, CA: Jossey–Bass.

Note: About 70% of this chapter was taken from Alexander, 2001.

Chapter 10

Alexander, James A. 2002. *The State of S-Business: An International Report of Progress, Performance and Best Practices*. Ft. Myers, FL: AFSM International.

Alexander, James A., and Hordes, Mark. 2002. A quick guide to managing resistance to s-business change. *Sbusiness* (AFSM International), *26*, 11 (November/December), 13–14.

Pannone, Ron, Winby, Stuart, and Woolf, David. 1985. Commitment analysis: First step toward change, *Manager's Notebook* (American Productivity Center), *2*, 4 (December), 3.

Ulrich, David. 1997. *Human Resource Champions: The Next Agenda for Adding Value and Delivering Results.* Boston, MA: Harvard Business School Press.

Note: All the "Leading Change" section came from Alexander and Hordes, 2002.